JANUARY BIBLE STUDY 2016
Adult Personal Study Guide

SECOND CORINTHIANS

The Church's Ministry Handbook

LifeWay Press®
Nashville, TN

ISBN: 978-1-4300-3955-6
Item: 005717343

Subject Area: Bible Studies
Dewey Decimal Classification Number: 227.3
Subject Heading: N.T. 2 CORINTHIANS–STUDY \ CHURCH \ MINISTRY
Printed in the United States of America

LifeWay Christian Resources
One LifeWay Plaza
Nashville, TN 37234-0175

We believe that the Bible has God for its author; salvation for its end; and truth, without any mixture of error, for its matter and that all Scripture is totally true and trustworthy. To review LifeWay's doctrinal guidelines, please visit *www.lifeway.com/doctrinalguideline.*

Cover Image, Title Page Image, Contents Page Image, Chapter Beginnings Image, and Learning Activities Image: IStock Photo

Contents

Introduction: A Church in Corinth 4

Chapter 1 **The Relationship Aspect of Ministry**
2 Corinthians 1:1–2:13 10

Chapter 2 **The Transformational Nature of Ministry**
2 Corinthians 2:14–4:6 25

Chapter 3 **The Eternal Perspective of Ministry**
2 Corinthians 4:7–5:10 40

Chapter 4 **The Gospel Focus of Ministry**
2 Corinthians 5:11–7:16 54

Chapter 5 **The Financial Aspect of Ministry**
2 Corinthians 8:1–9:15 69

Chapter 6 **The Personal Challenges of Ministry**
2 Corinthians 10:1–13:14 83

INTRODUCTION

A Church in Corinth

The location of Corinth made it a strategic and desirable site for a city. Corinth was the sentry city of a four and one-half mile isthmus that bridged the Peloponnese and the mainland and separated the Saronic and Corinthian gulfs. Most ship traffic found it safer and easier to take the inland route through Corinth than to go around the Peloponnese. Thus, Corinth had a growing population and a regular flow of visitors.

The city had everything necessary to make it a prosperous and licentious one. It had a good supply of water from springs, a natural defense provided by the towering Acrocorinth, two harbors that controlled East-West commerce, and it hosted the Isthmian games, which ranked just below the Olympics in importance. A city like Corinth attracted inhabitants and guests like a modern day Las Vegas.

Corinth was destroyed by the Romans in 146 B.C. and lay dormant for about one hundred years until it was refounded as a Roman colony in 44 B.C. The Roman freedmen were the dominant group in Corinth and they brought with them their Roman gods and their culture. But the process of Hellenization (Greek influence) had already begun to impact Roman culture; and since Corinth was historically Greek, it maintained its ties with the Greek religion, philosophy, and art. Thus Corinth was a melting pot of religious practices from East and West. From the East came the mystery cults of Egypt and Asia; from Rome and Greece came the pantheon of gods. With the expulsion of the Jews from Rome by Claudius (Acts 18:2), Judaism with its peculiar belief that there was only one true God was added to the religious stew.

To add a little spice, God tossed into the stew the greatest missionary of the first century—the apostle Paul. He quickly established a friendship with Aquila and Priscilla, Jews from Rome, who shared his profession as a tent maker and his belief that Jesus was the Messiah. This church planter extraordinaire dedicated eighteen months to developing a Christian stronghold in this pivotal city (Acts 18:11).

The re-founded Corinth quickly developed an aristocracy based on wealth, which created a fierce entrepreneurial spirit in the city. Not everyone struck it rich

and there were thousands of artisans and slaves who made up the bulk of the population. Like many seaport towns, debauchery and religion flourished side by side. Corinth may not sound like the most receptive environment for church planting, but the gospel is good seed, and soon after Paul's arrival a thriving church was planted. As expected, the church reflected the makeup of the community. It seems to have been composed mostly of Gentiles from the lower socioeconomic strata; nevertheless, there were several wealthy families among the members. There were also a few leading Jews, including the leader of the local synagogue.

Above: The acropolis of ancient Corinth

ILLUSTRATOR PHOTO/ BOB SCHATZ (11/6/14)

Nothing Boring About this Church

The church at Corinth might be described by numerous terms, but "boring" would not be one of them. The lack of unity can be seen in the claims—"I'm with Paul," or "I'm with Apollos, or "I'm with Cephas," or "I'm with Christ" (1 Cor. 1:12). But disunity, while a critical issue, was only the tip of the iceberg. Some members of the church were engaged in a noisy court battle, which Paul declared "a moral failure" (6:7). People insisted on their own rights, whether it was the right to eat meat sacrificed to idols (chap. 8) or the right of the women to speak in the assembly with their heads uncovered (chap. 11). Some were scandalized by the news that a man was sleeping with his stepmother (5:1), while others saw such behavior as a sign of their advanced spirituality (5:2). The celebration of the Lord's Supper ended with some leaving hungry while the wealthier members were tipsy from too much wine (11:21).

Everyone seemed to be confused about the matter of spiritual gifts. It seems apparent that some members saw their abundance of gifts as sure proof of their spiritual ascendancy. Some may have claimed to speak the language of the angels (13:1). The exaggerated claims of these "spirituals" had apparently caused others to question whether they had any gifts. The church at Corinth was made up of zealous new believers who could be easily swayed by powerful teachers. This spiritual immaturity would, on occasion, cause them to abandon the sound doctrine Paul taught and follow after false teaching.

Paul's Departure and the First Letters

After 18 months in Corinth, Paul left for Asia to continue his missionary work. After Paul left, the church was led by Stephanas, Fortunatus, and Achaicus (1 Cor. 16:17). During Paul's absence other leaders visited Corinth. Some, like Apollos, augmented Paul's message by watering the seed Paul had sown (3:6). Others, however, seem to have created considerable confusion in relation to spiritual gifts and various moral issues.

Sometime after his departure, Paul wrote a letter to the Corinthians that no longer exists. We read about it in 1 Corinthians 5:9: "I wrote to you in a letter not to associate with sexually immoral people." Its contents were misunderstood, and that misunderstanding along with other concerns prompted the writing of 1 Corinthians. Paul had several sources of information which must have influenced the topics he chose to discuss in this lengthy letter. Members of Chloe's household brought Paul the disheartening news that quarrels existed and disunity reigned in the church (1:11-12). Paul had received a letter from the Corinthian church which sought clarification on issues related to his original teaching and other matters which had become divisive. Paul's response to those concerns begins in 7:1.

Corinth after First Corinthians

In 1 Corinthians 16:5-10 Paul told the Corinthians that he desired to visit them after he traveled through Macedonia and that he may possibly spend the winter with them (probably the winter of A.D. 55-56). He wanted to remain in Ephesus until Pentecost because a wide door for effective ministry had been opened to him even in the midst of opposition. It is possible, however, that Paul would send Timothy to visit Corinth. Therefore, he appealed that they treat Timothy with due respect and send him on his way in peace.

Paul's plans were quickly modified and he decided it would be necessary to visit Corinth both on his way to Macedonia and again on his return from Macedonia. After the second of these two visits, he would then set sail for Judea to deliver the collection for the saints in Jerusalem (2 Cor. 1:15-16). However, Paul once again found that it was impossible to carry out this modified plan because of "affliction that took place in Asia" (v. 8). While we don't know the details of this affliction, we do know that Paul feared for his life (v. 9). A second issue that led to this further modification of his plans was the news of further trouble in Corinth which called for an urgent visit.

We must assume that 1 Corinthians had not been as effective as Paul had wished in dealing with issues that were causing confusion and division in Corinth. Further it appears that Timothy had not been sufficiently bold to enforce Paul's instructions. It is possible that Timothy may have brought back a discouraging report that convinced Paul that only a confrontational visit from Paul could resolve the tension and quell the rebellion in Corinth. Paul made a brief second visit which is referred to in 2 Corinthians 13:2 as one in which he warned them to deal with persons who had sinned by demanding proof that Christ is speaking through him. This visit was painful and humiliating for Paul and his converts in Corinth (2 Cor. 2:1). After that visit, Paul apparently fulfilled his plans to pass through Macedonia.

HOLMAN BIBLE PUBLISHERS

He then sent the Corinthians a letter which was written "with many tears out of an extremely troubled and anguished heart" (v. 4). Paul reminded them that the intent was not to hurt anyone, but to assure them of the abundant love he had for them. This letter, sent by the hand of Titus, not only assured them of his love, but it called on them to reaffirm their allegiance to him and to discipline those who had taken the lead in opposing him. This "tearful letter" has not been preserved and thus we can only reconstruct its contents by references to it in 2 Corinthians. Paul met Titus in Macedonia and his heart was put to rest when he received the news that the letter had been effective and that the Corinthians had renewed their love and loyalty to Paul (7:5-9). Paul immediately sent them the letter we call 2 Corinthians.

The Tenor and Content of Second Corinthians

As a whole, the tenor of 2 Corinthians is one of relief and deep affection. Since some persons were still upset by Paul's change of travel plans, he explained that his own circumstances along with his desire to avoid giving them further pain had caused him to alter his plans. Further, Paul was concerned that the Corinthians may have become overly zealous in their desire to punish the offender and he wanted to encourage them to forgive and restore the offender (2:5-11). To help the Corinthians better understand his work, he provided even greater detail concerning the trials and the joys of his apostolic ministry. We will discover in these sections some truths that will greatly encourage us in the work God has called us to embrace.

We will discover some truths that will greatly encourage us in the work God has called us to embrace.

During the time that relations had been strained between Paul and the Corinthians, he had not thought it prudent to follow up on the offering for the saints in Jerusalem, an issue which had been addressed in 1 Corinthians 16 and thus he devoted two chapters to discussing the value and joy of cooperative giving. He used the example of the Macedonians who gave out of their poverty to encourage them to give generously to help the saints in Jerusalem.

Chapters 10–13 of 2 Corinthians are a bit of an enigma. The reader is taken off guard by the change in tone and the extended defense Paul made of his apostolic authority and his denunciation of visitors to Corinth who attempted to undermine his authority. We will pay closer attention to this matter as we study those chapters in detail.

Pressing Questions for the Church Today

Second Corinthians can easily be called a handbook for church ministry. It answers pressing questions for the church today. *What is the ministry of the local church? What is the role of a church leader? What are the responsibilities of a church member? What are the right motivations for serving in the church and doing ministry? How do we deal with critics in ministry?* Paul's answers to such questions, while addressed to a specific church with unique problems in the first century, are as relevant today as they were 2,000 years ago. This study of Second Corinthians will remind us that the power for ministry is God working through us to accomplish His purposes and that the foundation and focus of all ministry is the gospel of Jesus Christ. Also, this study will challenge all believers to get involved in ministry and will help equip them to minister more effectively in their local churches.

Left: Temple of Apollo at Corinth

ILLUSTRATOR PHOTO/ AUDREY SMITH (35/43/88)

CHAPTER ONE

The Relational Aspect of Ministry

2 CORINTHIANS 1:1–2:13

"Thank you Father that you waste nothing. Amen!" Those words were uttered by a Catholic priest who had been asked to pray at a community-wide service in memory of those who were slain at the shooting at Wedgewood Baptist Church in 1999. The prayer was startling both in terms of its brevity and its profundity. I was president of Southwestern Baptist Theological Seminary in Fort Worth when the shootings that shocked the nation took place. I was scheduled to speak after that prayer and I must confess I was unprepared for such a short and meaningful epithet.

I am confident that many who had crowded into the football stadium at Texas Christian University were thinking about the tragic "waste" of life the shooting had caused. Newscasters had consistently given such an evaluation of the recent shooting. It certainly was a waste of young lives filled with potential, and I don't think the priest thought the shooting was not a tragedy. I think he was saying that God was bigger than the tragedy and was working to redeem it in ways we were not yet able to see. Dr. Jack McGorman preached in chapel at Southwestern the next week from Romans 8:28, echoing a similar theme: God is always at work in every situation in a redemptive fashion. The days, months, and years since the shooting have demonstrated that God wastes nothing.

Paul had been required to change his travel plans to return to Corinth because of trials he had faced in Asia, which he described as "a death sentence" (2 Cor. 1:9), and because of challenges presented by members of the church in Corinth. Yet, he affirmed that God was working in every circumstance both in his life and that of the believers in Corinth to bring about good.

Grace and Peace (2 Cor. 1:1-2)

As in all his letters, Paul followed the formula for the opening of a Greek letter, but modified it in such a way as to identify both the sender and the recipients

Above: Ancient harbor at Cencherae

ILLUSTRATOR PHOTO/ GB HOWELL (35/37/32)

by their distinctive Christian calling. Further, his greeting included a prayer that his recipients would receive God's grace and peace.

Paul described himself in verse 1 as **an apostle of Christ Jesus by God's will.** It is not insignificant that Paul spoke of his apostolic calling since his authority had been challenged by some in Corinth and would be defended vigorously in this letter. His calling was based on the will of God and that alone gave him authority for his ministry among the Corinthians.

In chapters 10–13, where we find Paul's extended defense of his ministry, he spoke of the "authority, which the Lord gave for building you up and not for tearing you down" (10:8). He described his work in Corinth as a ministry that God assigned to him (10:13), and indicated that all ministers should avoid commending themselves and seek rather the commendation of the Lord (10:18). These correctives were directed at those Paul called "super-apostles" (11:5) and the Corinthians who were so easily enticed by such men. They are also good instructions for all who would minister in Christ's name in every generation.

This letter was sent by Paul **and Timothy,** who is associated with Paul in the introduction of six different letters. In 1 Corinthians, Sosthenes is mentioned with Paul in the opening address rather than Timothy. From 1 Corinthians 4:17 we can surmise that Timothy had been sent to Corinth when 1 Corinthians was written, but Paul was uncertain he would reach Corinth by the time the letter arrived (see also 1 Cor. 16:10). It appears that Timothy rejoined Paul at Ephesus with the news that 1 Corinthians had not resolved the problems in Corinth and thus it was even more significant that Timothy should join Paul as the co-sender of this second letter.

The letter is addressed **to God's church at Corinth, with all the saints who are throughout Achaia.** The church is the local Christian community and clearly it is established by God and thus belongs to Him alone. The mention of the saints throughout Achaia indicates that Paul was aware and desirous that the Corinthian letters be read in churches beyond Corinth. Throughout his letters, Paul demonstrated an awareness that he was writing instructions which come from the Lord (see 1 Cor. 14:37) and thus instructive for every church.

We know of at least two church communities in Achaia. From Acts 17:34 we find that there were believers in Athens, and from Romans 16:1 we know of a church in Cenchreae. Paul addressed his recipients as "saints," those who were called by God and set apart for service to Him. Since we are God's church and His saints, this letter is as relevant to us and our church as it was to those who read it in the first century.

The church is the local Christian community and clearly it is established by God and thus belongs to Him alone.

Paul's greeting and prayer is that his recipients would receive **grace** and **peace.** Grace is the act of God which is the ground of all Christian existence. It is the corrective for all arrogant boasting in oneself. Peace is the outcome of God's redemptive act and is a state of total well-being which one gains only by God's grace. Such peace flows out of one's relationship with God and has a profound impact on one's relationship with his fellowman. Both come from God our Father and are mediated by the Lord Jesus Christ. God is the source and Christ is the means by which we receive grace and thus stand in peace.

Learning and Ministering from Life Experiences (2 Cor. 1:3-11)

Paul moved immediately from greeting to praise of God—**Praise the God and Father of our Lord Jesus Christ.** This brief benediction has profound theological content. God is known not only as the one true God, but He is known as the Father of the Son whom He sent into the world to redeem mankind. The Son is here described in three ways. In relationship to man and in sovereign authority, He is Lord; in His personal incarnation, He is Jesus; in His worldwide reign, and He is Christ (the anointed King).

Paul described God as **the Father of mercies and the God of all comfort.** The language appears to be that of Jewish liturgy and was a Hebrew way of saying that God is the all merciful Father. God's mercy is a consistent emphasis of Old Testament texts such as Psalm 103:13, Isaiah 51:12, and 66:13. From His inward attitude of mercy flows His outward action of comfort. God is the ultimate source of every act of encouragement and consolation for believers; however comfort may be mediated through human instruments. The theme of comfort dominates this opening section and sets the tone for the first nine chapters.

For the believer, every circumstance—good or bad—is used by God to equip us to minister to others.

Paul next spoke of his personal experience of having received comfort, which in turn, enabled him to comfort others. Paul twice mentioned his own affliction in language which is comprehensive—**all our affliction** and **any kind of affliction.** Paul had been sustained and strengthened by God, enabling him not simply to endure the tribulation, but to derive blessing from it. One blessing, which he will mention later (v. 9), was the move from self-reliance to God-reliance. Here, however, he focused on the blessing of developing the ability to comfort others in their hour of need. For the believer, every circumstance—good or bad—is used by God to equip us to minister to others.

While I was pastor in Norfolk, Virginia, my dad died of a brain tumor one year after detection and surgery. During that period, I was encouraged daily by the prayers and ministry of

From Suffering to Comfort

Read the following scenarios. Check each one that you believe would equip you to minister to someone in a similar situation:

____A cancer diagnosis
____Bankruptcy
____Drunk driving conviction
____Divorce
____Defaulting on a loan
____Parenting an adult practicing homosexuality
____School failure because of dyslexia
____Getting fired from a job
____The death of a spouse
____Teen pregnancy

Draw a circle around the sufferings that may be self-inflicted because of sin.

Is suffering the consequences of sin a valid way to become equipped for a ministry of comfort? Explain your answer.

the staff and church members. Years later, various people would tell me that during and after that time my preaching and ministry had a different level of empathy than they had felt prior to the affliction I experienced during my father's year of lingering death. What current event is God using to enable you to discover His sufficiency and to enable you to minister to others?

In verse 5 Paul identified his own affliction with **the sufferings of Christ.** Believers are united with Christ and thus, while serving Christ, will endure the same sufferings as Christ endured. In Philippians 3:10 Paul spoke of knowing both the power of His resurrection and the fellowship of His sufferings. We are often guilty of desiring the power without experiencing the suffering. Further, the sufferings of the Christian are unique because they are not our own; they are the "sufferings of Christ." When Christians suffer on earth, Christ continues to suffer (see Acts 9:4). But here is a profound miracle—when sufferings overflow, **so through Christ our comfort also overflows.** Paul's sufferings were in one sense redemptive because they brought comfort to his converts.

Paul continued the theme of ministry flowing out of one's personal experience. He boldly declared that his afflictions were for the **comfort and salvation** of the Corinthians (2 Cor. 1:6 and see also Col. 1:24). The Corinthians, seeing the nobility of Paul's response to his own suffering, would be encouraged when they themselves were called upon to suffer. Paul's hope that the Corinthians would stand true to their Christian commitment was firm (2 Cor. 1:7) because it was based on the very nature of God who is "the Father of mercies and the God of all comfort" (v. 3). His personal story of suffering and deliverance should give the Corinthians comfort and hope. Therefore, in the next several verses he shared some of the details of his suffering while in Asia.

Paul described his experience in very graphic language which indicates the severity of the event. **We were completely overwhelmed—beyond our strength—so that we even despaired of life.** The word picture is that of a beast of burden that is crushed beneath a heavy load and has been taxed beyond endurance.

If Paul was referring to the riot which ensued during his ministry in Ephesus (Acts 19:23-41), then the actual events

Below: The theater at Ephesus was built in the 3rd century B.C. Through the years it was modified until it reached its final form during the reign of the emperor Trajan (A.D. 98-117). The theater had seating capacity for 24,000. This is the site of the riot mentioned in Acts 19:23-41.

ILLUSTRATOR PHOTO/ TOM HOOKE (66/6/6)

must been more dangerous than Luke indicated in his brief account. Some think that the reference to **a death sentence within ourselves** indicates Paul suffered from a serious physical illness. If we take into account Paul's testimony in 2 Corinthians 11:28, we can further suggest that the rebellion of some in Corinth had caused Paul much anguish of soul. In truth, it may well have been a combination of all these factors. Our affliction often comes when pressures come from every side at once.

Paul celebrated not only his physical deliverance, but the life lesson he learned. While he was utterly helpless, taxed beyond his physical abilities, he had abandoned all self-reliance and placed his full trust in **God who raises the dead.** When we face death or other events that are beyond human solution, we recognize the limits of self-confidence and turn to God for true confidence and security. Why is it easier to celebrate the historical truth of the resurrection than it is to appropriate the reality of resurrection power for daily living?

Like Paul, our total reliance on God grows as we daily experience His power to deliver us. Paul now fully understood that God is pre-eminently the God who raises the dead. God not only raised Jesus from the dead; He raises men from the death caused by sin to a life of righteousness. At the general resurrection He will deliver us again. Therefore, in keeping with His own nature, God delivered Paul from **such a terrible death,** a death that seemed imminent and terrible, a death which would cut short his ministry. Paul's present deliverance had confirmed that he could place his hope in God alone.

Paul now paused to celebrate the role of prayer which he referred to as **the gift that came to us through the prayers of many.** He invited the Corinthians to **join in helping us by your prayers.** There is no limit to the power of intercessory prayer, and thus when it is answered there is a spontaneous outburst of praise and thanksgiving which ultimately gives glory to God. Prayer illustrates the unique interrelationship between God's sovereign activity on earth and man's responsible participation. Through corporate intercessory prayer we cooperate with one another and with God in the expansion of His kingdom on earth.

Through corporate intercessory prayer we cooperate with each other and with God in the expansion of His kingdom on earth.

The Minister's Conduct in the World (2 Cor. 1:12-14)

Paul now spoke of the motivation and conduct for all authentic ministry. It should be characterized by sincerity and purity, based on grace, and lead to authentic pride in the day of the Lord. Since all believers are called to ministry, this section provides invaluable helps for us in our daily ministry.

Contrary to what his critics may have been saying, Paul was justifiably proud that his behavior in the world **and especially toward you** was based on **God-given sincerity and purity.** The word *boast* is a common word in both the Corinthian letters, occurring 10 times in 1 Corinthians and 29 times in 2 Corinthians. The Corinthians often boasted in the wrong things such as human leaders, their supposed freedom, and their powerful gifts. Paul, however, boasted in grace alone. It was God's grace that had enabled him to minister with sincerity and purity in spite of the challenging circumstances he faced.

The derivation of the word *sincerity* is uncertain, but it may refer to the process of rolling and shaking in a sieve so that what remains is unadulterated. In 1 Corinthians 5:8 Paul used the same word to refer to the "unleavened bread of sincerity." It may also refer to what is unstained when examined in full sunlight. In that case, Paul would be saying that his character and behavior would stand the test of the searching gaze of God.[1]

Paul did not minister with **fleshly wisdom** but functioned by God's grace alone. Fleshly wisdom was a common theme of the first letter. Paul began that letter by contrasting the wisdom of the wise with the foolishness of the cross (1 Cor. 1:18-25). He was forced to bring correction when some members arrogantly ate idol meat based on their "knowledge" which was incomplete, yet had inflated them with pride (8:1-3). Paul did not base his ministry on human wisdom or strength, but he was controlled and empowered by the grace of God—it alone was the dominating factor of his life.

Paul's reference to the sincerity and purity of his ministry seems to have been elicited by the accusation of his opponents that he had misled them about his travel plans and thus his letters and actions contradicted one another. Paul affirmed that his written correspondence had the same integrity as the rest of his conduct. He desired that they would **understand completely** since they had only **partially understood.** Paul affirmed that his change in travel plans were not based on human reasoning but on God's grace and the direction of the Spirit (vv. 15-22).

Paul reminded them that he and his companions would be their reason for pride, **as you are ours,** in the day of our Lord Jesus. Paul could boast of the Corinthians as the fruit

of his ministry, which means that they owed their faith to his effective ministry in Corinth. In truth, the status of each was confirmed by that of the other. They should not disparage his apostolic work since they were the fruit of that work. Can your character, motives, and ministry be described by the words *sincerity* and *purity*? Do you often find that you rely more on fleshly wisdom and human strength than you do the grace of God?

Say What You Mean and Mean What You Say (2 Cor. 1:15-22)

In 1 Corinthians 16:5 Paul indicated that he would visit the Corinthians after he had passed through Macedonia. In this context, he indicated that after the writing of 1 Corinthians he had to alter his plans. He would cross straight from Ephesus to Corinth and then go to Macedonia, **with your help,** and then return to Corinth after his visit to Macedonia. The phrase *with your help* may refer to the collection for the relief of the saints in Jerusalem, a task they had not completed. We must assume that this plan was originally communicated with them before Paul found it necessary to revise it once again. His original intention behind the double visit was to give them a **double benefit.**

Paul posed rhetorical questions which anticipated a clear and resounding no in response. When he planned to make a double visit was he being **irresponsible?** It seems that some were making such accusations, but the clear answer was *no.* Did he make his plans based on human logic; like an unregenerate man would do? Was he ready to say "yes" one day and then "no" the next based on pure whim?

Paul clearly had a change of plans, but the change was not based on **purely human** reasoning; his plans were not self-centered. A self-centered person is undependable because he will alter his plans based on that which is most convenient to him. The suggestion that Paul was self-centered was so abhorrent to the apostle that he affirmed his integrity with a solemn assertion—**As God is faithful.** Paul was not the sole witness to his integrity; he called upon God who is faithful. Paul, like the God he served, said what he meant and meant what he said. A lack of personal integrity would call into question the gospel he preached.

Paul could never minister as a **yes and no** man for Jesus whom he and his colleagues preached was the embodiment of the divine Yes. **For every one of God's promises is "Yes" in Him.** All the promises God made to the patriarchs and prophets have found their ultimate "yes" in Jesus. Because Christ is the "yes" to God's promises, Christians can respond in worship with **Amen,** meaning "this is truth." Paul, Silvanus, and Timothy had preached the gospel which was the very basis for their Christian existence. Every time they said amen they were acknowledging the truth of the gospel Paul preached. With so much at stake, Paul would never deceive them about insignificant matters such as the change of travel plans.

All who are concerned with the integrity of the gospel—both preacher and respondent—need to live with the utmost integrity in their personal lives.

All who are concerned with the integrity of the gospel—both preacher and respondent—need to live with the utmost integrity in their personal lives. Once again notice that the apostle's standing was integrally intertwined with that of his converts. The word *strengthens* was common in commercial and legal usage and can also mean "to confirm." God alone can verify or confirm the integrity of the work of the minister and the response of the hearer. Not only has God confirmed us, He has **anointed us.** *Anointed* refers to the simultaneous call to salvation and ministry. God saves us to join Him in His redemptive work and then guarantees a successful mission.

Left: Map of Achaia and surrounding area.

HOLMAN BIBLE PUBLISHERS

Below: Stamped jar handle from Lachish dating to the reign of King Hezekiah (late 8th century B.C.). The handle is impressed with the seal "lamelekh Hebron."

ILLUSTRATOR PHOTO/ BRENT BRUCE/ EREZT ISRAEL MUSEUM/ TEL AVIV, ISRAEL (60/9336)

God sets His seal upon us, marking us out as those who belong to Him, serve Him, and who are eternally the objects of His loving care. **Sealed** comes from commercial imagery. It was a mark of ownership used to assure that a document was authentic. It was also used to assure that goods in transit were not tampered with, but had arrived intact. We are His and we will arrive before Him fully intact. To assure our hearts we have been given the Holy Spirit who is our **down payment.** This assures us that all will be paid in full (see Eph. 1:14). How does your personal integrity, or lack thereof, have an impact on your ministry and the gospel you affirm?

Minister Out of the Overflow of Love (2 Cor. 1:23–2:4)

To assure the Corinthians that his change of plans had not come about because of any selfish motivation, Paul called on **God as a witness.** His reason for the change of plans was not based on a lack of integrity; it arose from love and pastoral concern. If he had carried out his original plans when the community was in turmoil concerning his apostolic authority, he would have caused much pain. His love prompted him to spare them such an encounter.

It is not that Paul was a tyrant; even an apostle had no right to dictate when it came to a matter of one's personal faith or conscience. He was their minister and friend, working with them for their joy. They stood by faith and it was Paul's singular desire that they share equally in the liberty of the Spirit, but they must do so through disciplined corporate living. It was for this reason that Paul made up his mind **not to come to you on another painful visit.** The use of *another* seems to suggest that a painful visit unrecorded in Acts had occurred since the writing of 1 Corinthians. It must have been the visit mentioned in 2 Corinthians 13:2.

Paul had already indicated that his desire was to work with them to promote **joy.** Any suggestion that he desired to cause them pain by his visit would be foolish and counterproductive since the only ones who could cheer him up would be those upon whom he had inflicted **pain**. A minister may, under exceptional circumstances, find it his duty to cause pain through discipline. But he does so out of pure motives and with a positive goal in sight. Paul expressed confidence in them and affirmed that his joy would be shared by them (v. 3).

Authentic ministry—whether painful or joyous—must flow from a heart of love.

To spare them another painful visit, Paul wrote them a tearful letter. Once again, it appears that this letter has not survived. He desired that the letter would spare them any other painful visits. A visit that transpired during their rebellious state would produce sorrow for all. According to 2 Corinthians 7:8, the letter must have had its intended impact. But writing such a letter had been no easy task—**I wrote**

to you with many tears out of an extremely troubled and anguished heart. While it was written in much pain; it was written from the context of **abundant love.** Authentic ministry—whether painful or joyous—must flow from a heart of love.

Be Ready to Forgive (2 Cor. 2:5-11)

It seems likely that much of the trouble at Corinth had been caused by a particular offender, known by Paul but not specified by name. Likely, he had verbally attacked and insulted Paul, either while Paul was present among them or during his absence. While some have identified this man with the offender put out of the church for immorality (1 Cor. 5), that seems unlikely because Paul was not speaking of a moral issue here but one which included a personal attack on the authority of the apostle, and thus had created division in the church.

Paul, however, was not primarily concerned about any personal pain that had been caused by this individual. In truth, this offender has caused pain **to all of you.** The church is the body of Christ, and when one member suffers the entire body suffers (see 1 Cor. 12:26). The sin of this individual had created such disunity that it had impacted the effectiveness of the church in fulfilling its mission. So it is no exaggeration to say that the pain intended for Paul alone had caused pain to the entire church. Do we understand that our sinful and divisive behavior has corporate dimensions?

Our sinful and divisive behavior has corporate dimensions.

Paul had learned from Titus that the Corinthians, moved by the painful letter, had taken appropriate steps by punishing the offender. **By the majority** may suggest that a minority of members had dissented, desiring more or less punishment. In any case, Paul believed that the punishment meted out was **sufficient for that person.** The Corinthians must now move on to the more gracious task of restoration. All church discipline should be restorative and not punitive in nature.

Three steps are described in the process of restoration—**forgive, comfort,** and confirm your **love.** Since the individual had repented, the church members individually and

Damage Control

It may be easier than you realize to damage one's reputation as a Christian because of lack of integrity in the small things. Put a checkmark beside the items below that would make you question a leader if you discovered that person doing one of these:

____ keeping the extra change when overpaid
____ making personal copies at work
____ attending movies with questionable messages or images
____ embellishing a resume
____ repeatedly overdrawing one's bank account
____ carrying a large debt load
____ belittling or berating one's spouse in front of others
____ consistently neglecting to show up for a child's sports or school activities
____ refusing to give money to a beggar when asked
____ not making time to make a new neighbor's acquaintance

Draw a circle around the items of which you're guilty.

If you were to rate your integrity on a scale of 1 (poor) to excellent (5), how would you assess yourself? ______

corporately must extend and express forgiveness. Since an awareness of sin causes godly sorrow, the repentant church member would need to be comforted. If comfort does not accompany forgiveness, **this one may be overwhelmed by excessive grief**. Without comfort, grief over one's sin can have a crushing effect rather than a remedial one. It can drive the offender into despair and isolation, when what he needs is encouragement and community.

For this reason, Paul called upon the Corinthians to **reaffirm** their **love to him.** *Reaffirm* has the sense of "ratify" and thus it is a public affirmation of a decision already rendered. (See Gal. 3:15.) All future dealings must be characterized by brotherly love. In this step, it may be appropriate that the individual be restored to a ministry position within the church.

The letter mentioned in verse 9 was likely the tearful letter written between First and Second Corinthians. Forgiveness, restoration, and a reaffirmation of love would be wholly consistent with what Paul had in view when he wrote the letter.

Paul had no desire for personal vindication—his desire was to protect the church, prove the obedience of the Corinthians, and restore a brother. Their total obedience had demonstrated their character and thus Paul agreed fully with the church decision that the penitent should be forgiven. Paul had forgiven the offender for the good of the church (**for you).** The phrase, ***in the presence of Christ,*** could mean with Christ's authority or in light of Christ's forgiveness of all. It may also indicate Christ's real presence when believers assemble as His body.

The adversary likes nothing better than to sow discord among the brethren.

Verse 11 explains more fully what Paul meant by the phrase *for you*. If the offender remained unforgiven and was driven to despair after having repented, Satan would have an **advantage** over both the offender and the church. Satan could destroy the individual with unresolved sorrow and thus keep him from effective future ministry. Further, prolonged punishment or ostracism could lead to tension and division in the church, thus impacting its ministry. The adversary likes nothing better than to sow discord among the brethren.

Personal Reflection

1. What experience of comfort have you received that might enable you to minister to others?

2. How can personal sin impact the effectiveness of a church's ministry?

3. Do you think the church should have clear guidelines for discipline and restoration? What do you think those guidelines should be?

A CLOSER LOOK

God's Discipline

Discipline is not a topic we enjoying discussing, particularly when it comes to the Christian life. Hebrews 12 contains several practical suggestions about how we should respond when the Lord brings discipline into our personal lives. First, God says that we should not take it "lightly" (Heb. 12:5). God's discipline is a serious matter and thus we must embrace it with appropriate gravity. Second, we should not "faint" (v. 5). He will not bring discipline into our lives that we cannot bear. Third, we should view discipline in the context of our relationship with God as Father. It is a sure indication we are God's children and clear evidence of His love for us (vv. 6-8). Fourth, we are fully assured that every aspect of God's discipline is for our benefit, and will allow us to share His character (vv. 10-11).

1. R.V.G. Tasker, *2 Corinthians: Tyndale New Testament Commentaries* (London, The Tyndale Press, 1969), 45.

CHAPTER TWO

The Transformational Nature of Ministry

2 CORINTHIANS 2:14–4:6

Childhood memories are fascinating. I grew up in Thomasville, North Carolina. Main street was one sided because a train track ran through the middle of town. I loved walking down the street gazing into the display windows of the stores, such as Belks and Roses dime store. I was never quite sure how the store owner managed to put just the item in the window that I "needed" or "wanted," but it seemed to happen with unfailing regularity. I just had to have the shiny red bike prominently displayed in the Belks' window.

I loved to go with my parents to grandma Kincaid's house. As soon as I entered the house, I was drawn to the kitchen by the smell of biscuits baking in a wood stove. As I write this, the smell and the memories of that house come flooding back to my consciousness.

Display windows and fragrant smells have more in common than you might think. They both serve to create a desire and a hunger in the one who sees or smells the item. Paul spoke of his ministry as a display and a fragrance. We must ask ourselves are we like a display window and a fragrance which draws people to Christ?

Minister with Integrity and Fragrance (2 Cor. 2:14-17)

In verses 12-13, Paul indicated that he had left Troas where a door of effective ministry had been opened by the Lord. As the months passed without any word from Titus concerning the affairs of the church in Corinth, Paul had "no rest in his spirit" (v. 13). Although he could have remained in Troas with profitable ministry, he left for Macedonia where he would meet Titus. Paul hit the pause button on the story of his travel narrative, which will be taken up again in 7:5, to describe his relief and thanksgiving based on the encouraging report he had received from Titus.

The linking word **but** is a strong adversative. In spite of the fears, anxieties, and challenges of ministry, Paul began his celebration with a simple but profound, **thanks be to God.** He utilized two related images to speak of his ministry. The first is from the military; it is the picture of a general leading his captives in a triumphal procession. Paul, however, was not a captive in the procession; he was one of the field officers sharing in the general's great victory. It was clear to Paul that despite occasional setbacks, Christ's triumphal procession moves steadily across the world to the ends of the earth **(every place).**

The phrases **the aroma of the knowledge of Him** and **fragrance of Christ** may be an allusion to the perfumes that were sprinkled along the victor's route, creating an event that was replete with sight, sound, and smell. The fragrance of ministry is the aroma of the knowledge of Him. When the gospel of God's redeeming love is declared, it emits a sweet fragrance. Sinful man is given the remedy against sin and death. The responder, who was once alienated and without hope, now has the joy of knowing Christ in personal relationship.

When the gospel of God's redeeming love is declared, it emits a sweet fragrance.

Nothing delights the heart of God more than when the gospel is declared and therefore those who proclaim it are the aroma of Christ to God. Stop a moment and meditate on that truth! How does it make you feel to know that you are the aroma of Christ to God when you declare the gospel?

The clear and fragrant declaration of the gospel does not mean that all will respond. The perfumes that strewed the path of the triumphal procession increased the joy of the victorious participants, but for those who were to be executed at the end of the procession, they were a fragrance from death to death.[1] For those who join the triumphal procession by responding in faith to the fragrant message, the apostolic witnesses are **an aroma of life leading to life,** but for those who reject their message they are **an aroma of death leading to death.**

The message of the gospel comes from life and leads to life; it tells of life and leads to life eternal (see Rom. 6:22). But that which is life-giving in nature, when rejected, becomes a scent of death which inevitably leads to eternal death. What is intended to be a medicine that heals becomes a poison that kills. All are sinners by nature and by choice and the wages of sin is death. Thus when the sweet fragrance of the gospel is rejected it becomes the scent of death. The same idea is present in the imagery of Jesus as a cornerstone for the one who believes and a rock of stumbling for those who disobey the message (1 Pet. 2:6-8).

With so much at stake in the preaching of the gospel, Paul must pause and wonder—**And who is competent for this?** Paul's opponents prided themselves in their self-sufficiency, but the anticipated response to Paul's question is that no one is competent in his own unaided strength. Our competence for ministry is never in or of ourselves; it comes from God's call and empowering.

Our competence for ministry is never in or of ourselves; it comes from God's call and empowering.

Paul now compared his ministry and that of his companions with that of **the many who market God's message for profit.** Some commentators believe that the imagery comes from the market place where the dishonest merchant would adulterate his goods and thus achieve excessive profit. In that case, Paul was questioning not only the motives of the many, likely a reference to his opponents, but also the message.

In direct contrast, Paul and his companions were men of sincerity. Both their message and their motives were pure. Paul boldly declared, **We speak with sincerity in Christ, as**

Left: Glass perfume bottles dating from the 1st-2nd centuries A.D

ILLUSTRATOR PHOTO/ BRITISH MUSEUM/ LONDON (31/13/49)

from God and before God. We might paraphrase, "We speak, aware of Christ's presence, as God's representatives who are commissioned by God and thus accountable to Him." For Paul, any tampering with the message or compromise of his mission was unthinkable.

Minister with Competence (2 Cor. 3:1-6)

Having introduced the theme of competence, Paul continued with this thought in mind. He began the discussion with two questions which are virtually rhetorical in nature. **Are we beginning to commend ourselves again? Or do we need, like some, letters of recommendation to you or from you?** The questions taken together are somewhat ironic. Surely, Paul did not need to introduce himself and his ministry to the Corinthians again. He could not imagine that the Corinthians had already forgotten his ministry and needed any further credentials. Surely they didn't need a letter of recommendation from their founder.

The use of letters of recommendation was widespread during antiquity. Paul did not object to the practice, which could be useful to both the minister and the church. In fact, Paul commended Phoebe to the church in Rome (Rom. 16:1), the messengers who would take the offering to Jerusalem (2 Cor. 8:16-24), and Tychicus who was the bearer of the letter to Colossae (Col. 4:7). He apparently required all the churches who would participate in the offering for Jerusalem to send a letter of recommendation with the individual who would accompany the gift (1 Cor. 16:3).

Paul, however, had never made use of testimonials written by other Christians and he certainly had no intention to write one in his own interest. Further, it would be absurd to think that the church at Corinth would require such since he planted the church. This reference to letters of commendation does indicate that he was aware that teachers had arrived in Corinth, fortifying their teaching with such letters. Later, he would speak of men who commend themselves (2 Cor. 10:12) and conclude: "For it is not the one commending himself who is approved, but the one the Lord commends" (10:18).

In truth, Paul did have a letter of recommendation—**You yourselves are our letter.** The Corinthians church was a letter written by Christ. Paul's converts were his letter which fully affirmed the genuine nature of his ministry activity. As such, they were written on his heart. In spite of the pain they had afflicted on the apostle, as his dear children, they were always on his heart.

The Corinthians were a living letter, and as such they could be **recognized and read by everyone.** The gospel, when fully received, will produce a radical change which will manifest itself in the lives of men and women so that it can be read and recognized by others. So the greater burden of authenticity was borne by the Corinthians, not the apostle. The question they should have been asking themselves was, when their lives were read, did they reflect the transforming power of the gospel? We might ask the same question of ourselves.

Did they reflect the transforming power of the gospel? We might ask the same question of ourselves.

The Corinthians were not simply Paul's letter of recommendation; they were Christ's letter, **not written with ink but with the Spirit of the living God.** The letter was produced by Paul, which may either suggest that he was the messenger who delivered it or the transcriber who took down the words that came from God and were delivered by the Spirit.

Paul contrasted **ink** with **Spirit,** and **stone tablets** with **hearts of flesh.** Both reinforce the idea that the Corinthian believers were a living letter. The mention of the writing by the Spirit prompted Paul to recall the divine writing at Mount Sinai, when Moses received the two stone tablets written with the finger of God (Ex. 31:18). This thought led to an extended contrast between a ministry of death and a ministry of life.

In verses 4-6, Paul answered the question he posed in 2 Corinthians 2:16 related to competency for ministry. His confidence was **toward God through Christ.** It was not based on his own natural abilities nor on his personal reputation, but solely on the activity of the risen Christ. His confidence was toward God and therefore it would stand up to God's scrutiny. In spite of the difficulties and misunderstandings, Paul was confident in his ministry because his competence was from God. No minister, by unaided intellect, could ever devise a message as gracious as God or a plan as powerful as the simple preaching of the gospel. The call to ministry is always accompanied by divine enabling.

The call to ministry is always accompanied by divine enabling.

Verse 6 begins with a simple affirmation that has profound implications—**He has made us competent to be ministers of a new covenant.** Paul distinguished between the new covenant and the old by using the contrasting categories of Spirit and letter and life and death. The Mosaic covenant required perfect obedience to laws and regulations external to men

Competency Core

Paul assured us that we are competent ministers of the new covenant. Check the ministry below that you feel competent to perform.

___Tell someone how Jesus changed your life.
___Pray with a dying friend at the hospital.
___Comfort a grieving parent who just lost a child.
___Lead a lost person in the sinner's prayer.
___Pray for a friend who is out of work.
___Explain how to be born again.
___Share a meal with a visiting family.
___Preach at a jail.
___Lead a Bible study in your workplace.
___Encourage a friend who is depressed.

If there are areas in which you feel inadequate, how could you address them?

which all men found impossible. Therefore, all mankind became liable to the penalty of their disobedience which was death. Thus it could be said that the letter kills. The new covenant, however, is based on Christ's death on the cross as the sole means by which sinful mankind could be reconciled to God as they responded to the life-giving witness of the Spirit.

It is wholly in keeping with this new covenant that God would use persons revitalized by the Spirit and thus made competent as ministers of such a covenant. Once again, the contrast is between human initiate and divine action. Paul's competence was found in the latter.

Minister with Boldness (2 Cor. 3:7-18)

Paul continued the comparison between the new covenant and the old using graphic terms such as **ministry of death** and **ministry of condemnation,** in contrast to **ministry of the Spirit** and **ministry of righteousness.** Based on the affirmation that the letter kills (3:6) Paul referred to ministry under the law, which was **chiseled in letters on stone,** as a ministry of death. The law killed in the sense that natural man could never fully obey it. But that does not mean that the law was evil. It reflects the character of God and therefore it **came with glory.**

Paul provided a commentary on the account of the giving of the law as recorded in Exodus 34:29-35 to show the transient nature of the glory that accompanied the giving of the law. When Moses first descended from Mount Sinai with the tablets in his hand, his face shone as a result of having spoken with God. Aaron and the Israelites were afraid to come near to Moses. While Moses spoke to the Israelites, he removed the veil so they could see the reflected glory. When he had finished speaking he replaced the veil. Any time Moses went before the Lord he would remove the veil and, after the Israelites had seen the reflected glory, he would again replace the veil.

Paul used this story to establish two truths about the giving of the law. The law, though it led to death, was a revelation of God's glory. Second, the law could not be the ultimate disclosure of God's glory or His redemptive purposes because the glory was **a fading glory,** a glory which was transient. Paul inferred from the account in Exodus that the longer Moses was absent from the divine presence, the more the brightness of God's glory faded from his countenance. If the glory of the law was a transient one, he questioned—**How will the ministry of the Spirit not be more glorious?** The ministry of the Spirit is both permanent and final.

The law is referred to here as **the ministry of condemnation** because it condemns the lawbreaker who is unable, in human strength, to live up to its demands. Nonetheless, as is evident from the glory reflected on the face of Moses, the ministry of the law was inaugurated with God's glory. The **ministry of righteousness** refers to the new covenant, under which man is now put right with God because the demands of the law have been satisfied in Christ who inaugurated the new covenant. The gospel is the message of righteousness because it proclaims God's justifying action through faith in Jesus Christ, the righteousness of God, for all who believe in Him.

Paul affirmed that the ministry of righteousness **overflows with even more glory.** So great is the difference between the glory of the law and the glory of righteousness that the old covenant appears not to have been glorious at all. A candle may appear bright in a darkened room until its light is eclipsed by the brilliance of electric lighting, in which case its light is barely noticeable. Paul returned to the matter of the **fading** of the glory on the face of Moses to illustrate the transience of the old covenant as contrasted with the permanence of the new. Because the new covenant is permanent, it has an abiding glory. **What endures will be even more glorious.**

The hope that springs forth from the assurance of the unfading nature of the gospel, which he and his associates have been commissioned to preach, gave them **great boldness.** Paul's message had been characterized by boldness or frankness because he was certain of his mission and his message. The word ***hope*** indicates that as great as the glory is which had been reflected in his ministry, the glory of God had not yet been fully displayed. That full display awaits the return of the Lord. But Paul's hope was so well founded it was a certainty that gave him boldness in ministry.

Paul contrasted his boldness with that of Moses who had to put a veil over his face to keep the Israelites from seeing the end of the glory which was fading away. The fading glory was not due to any failure on Moses' part; it was inherent in the very nature of the covenant he mediated which was destined to fade away when Christ came to fulfill the law. In the same way that the sacrifices of bulls and goats were replaced with the perfect sacrifice of Christ, the ministry of the law was replaced by the ministry of righteousness.

The Old Testament Scriptures are only fully intelligible when seen and understood in the light of the coming of Christ.

The Israelites' inability to see the fading glory on Moses' face is treated as a parable which depicted the inability of the Jews of Paul's day to realize the transitory and preparatory character of the Mosaic order or to see the unfading glory of the gospel. The phrase ***their minds were closed*** speaks of spiritual blindness of the Israelites. A similar spiritual blindness could be witnessed in Paul's day when the old covenant was read in the synagogue and the Jews failed to see that Jesus the Christ was the fulfillment of the Old Testament law and promises. Thus it was true that the veil remains, but not over the face of Moses. Now it covered the faces of the Jews who should have realized that the Old Testament Scriptures are only fully intelligible when seen and understood in the light of the coming of Christ. The veil of blindness **is set aside only in Christ.**

Paul spoke to the present day tragedy—**Even to this day, whenever Moses is read, a veil lies over their hearts.** There is hope! **But whenever a person turns to the Lord, the veil is removed.** The imagery is once again borrowed from the Exodus narrative. When Moses went before the Lord, the veil was removed temporarily. Now that Christ the Lord has come, it is possible for the veil to be permanently removed. Thus when a Jew, or Gentile for that matter, turns to Christ and sees in Him the fulfillment of the Mosaic Law, the veil is removed.

Paul affirmed that **the Lord,** who has already been shown to be **Christ,** in whom the Old Testament finds its fulfillment, is also the Spirit. Throughout this section Paul has maintained that the ministry of the Spirit produces life (v. 6) and thus is **more glorious** (v. 8) in nature. Now he affirmed that the Lord and the Spirit are one in the same sense that Jesus could say that He and the Father were one (John 10:30). It is the Spirit who brings conviction of sin and conveys to the believer the life of the risen Christ. The ministry of the Spirit produces freedom. He gives freedom from every kind of bondage—law (Gal. 5:18), sin (Rom. 7:5-6), fear (Rom. 8:15), and corruption (Rom. 8:21,23).[2]

Paul concluded this section by speaking of the transformation which comes to all believers through the ministry of the Lord who is the Spirit. It is affected daily in the lives of those who have no veil between them and the Lord. That veil is removed when they turn to the Lord (v. 16). Moses briefly reflected the glory of the Lord when in His presence, but that glory quickly faded when he was absent from God's presence. Now, by the ministry of the Spirit, God is continually present with us and in us. Through Christ, the veil has been removed and we not only reflect God's glory, but we are being transformed from glory to glory into the same image.

Now, by the ministry of the Spirit, God is continually present with us and in us.

As Christians behold the image of Christ, they are transformed by that glory and thus begin to reflect God's glory more clearly in their own lives. **From glory to glory** means from one stage of glory to another as the Spirit molds us into the image of Christ. The word translated **transformed** is the same word used by Paul in Romans 12:2 where he spoke of transformation by the renewing of the mind. It is also used in Mark 9:2 and Matthew 17:2 to speak of the transfiguration of Jesus. This ministry of transformation is from the Lord who is the Spirit. Is there any clear evidence that your life is being transformed from glory to glory?

Minister with an Open Display of Truth (2 Cor. 4:1-6)

Since Paul and his colleagues had a ministry which was a ministry of righteousness, superior to that of Moses, and overflowing with God's glory, they would not give up. Paul understood he was the recipient of such a calling and opportunity only because of God's mercy. In one of Paul's final letters, a pastoral letter addressed to Timothy, he wrote about the mercy he had received in his appointment to ministry.

> I give thanks to Christ Jesus our Lord, who has strengthened me, because He considered me faithful, appointing me to the ministry—one who was formerly a blasphemer, a persecutor, and an arrogant men. But I received mercy because I acted out of ignorance in unbelief (1 Tim. 1:12-13).

Because of the greatness of the task and the depth of the mercy received, **we do not give up.** So glorious is the mission received, it outweighs all distractions, inconveniences, and suffering. When we read the list of challenges Paul faced, as enumerated in 2 Corinthians 11:22-28, we have a more complete understanding of his commitment not to shrink from his duties no matter the cost. The magnitude of the ministry coupled with his certain hope kept him faithful to the task. When you face discouragement in ministry, do you focus on challenges faced or mercy received?

So glorious is the mission received, it outweighs all distractions, inconveniences, and suffering.

Paul did not rely on **shameful secret things.** In other words, he did not resort to disgraceful and underhanded techniques. His ministry was not characterized by deceit which would distort God's message. The same word is used here that is found in 2 Corinthians 11:3 to describe Satan's deception of Eve. Paul had such high regard for the integrity of his message that he would not dilute its severity to make himself popular, nor would he embellish it to make himself appear wiser. In no way would he falsify or compromise the simple truth of the gospel.

Paul lived and ministered in such an open and transparent way that he was willing to allow every man to decide about his integrity in their own conscience.

Not only had they heard the unadulterated truth from Paul, they had seen it displayed in his life and ministry. The Corinthians had sufficient evidence to make a sound judgment about Paul and his ministry. When you think about your life and ministry, can you describe it as an **open display of the truth**?

Paul may have been aware that some in Corinth were saying that his message was obscure or obtuse. Paul conceded that his message may be veiled to some, but the issue in that case is not with the messenger but with the hearer. Paul picked up once again the image of the veil that was the cause of Israel's rejection of the message of Christ (3:14-15). He also reminded them that, for those who were perishing, his ministry was a scent of death (2:16). For those who heard Paul with their ears but chose not to respond with their hearts, the message was veiled precisely because they were among the perishing.

Those perishing are in their present condition because **the god of this age has blinded the minds of the unbelievers** (4:4). The clear teaching of the New Testament is that Satan and his demons, though defeated at the cross, still have powerful influence in the present age. Jesus called Satan the "ruler of this world" (John 12:31, 14:30, and 16:11). John declared that the whole world is still under the sway of the evil one (1 John 5:19). Satan's work is to blind the minds of unbelievers so they cannot see the light of the gospel.

The light of the gospel overcomes darkness and spiritual blindness because it reveals the glory of Christ who is the image of God. The light of the gospel enables us to see the essential splendor of God in Christ; we can see Christ's God character. John opened his Gospel with the declaration that we now see the glory of God in His One and Only Son, full of grace and truth (John 1:14). In Jesus' prayer recorded in John 17, He prayed that on the cross and beyond the Father would glorify Him with His full pre-existent glory (v. 5). It was only after His suffering and death that Jesus entered fully into His glory (Luke 24:26).

The resurrected and glorified Lord appeared to Paul on the Damascus Road and changed his unbelief into belief. He was momentarily blinded physically that he might have spiritual sight. Paul had seen the earthly Jesus as a blasphemer, but now He saw Him as the Christ, **who is the image of God.**

In Jesus, the image of the likeness of God is fully present. Man was created in the image of God (Gen. 1:26), but through the fall that perfect image in man was distorted. Only one man who has inhabited earth fully displayed the image of God, and that was Jesus. Thus, He alone can restore sinful man to His image, transforming him from glory to glory (2 Cor. 3:18).

The authentic minister always wants to draw attention to Jesus and not himself.

While the events in Corinth made it necessary for Paul to answer his critics, he and his colleagues had no desire to proclaim themselves; their only desire was to proclaim Jesus Christ as Lord. The authentic minister always wants to draw attention to Jesus and not himself. Paul wanted them to see Jesus who is the crucified and risen Messiah (Christ). He desired that they know Him as Lord who demands total loyalty and obedience. If he declared anything about himself it was that he was their slave because of Jesus. The minister has an overriding loyalty to Christ. We are servants to others because we are a servant of Jesus Christ.

Ministry is every believers' mandate because God has shone in our hearts to enable us to see and reflect the light of the knowledge of God's glory in the face of Jesus Christ. What Paul had seen and heard on the Damascus road was

so overwhelming that it could never remain his own private possession. (See Gal. 1:15-16 and Acts 26:15-16.) Paul's heart was divinely illumined, enabling him to see who Jesus really is and that knowledge was his commission to become Christ's ambassador.

Ministry is every believers' mandate.

The only parallel to the action of the gospel penetrating the darkness of the sinful human heart is the dispersal of the darkness that once covered the surface of the watery depths (Gen. 1:2). In the first instance God spoke the light into existence; but through His Son He came as light. The Creator who overcame darkness with light in the first day of creation can subdue the darkness of sin that covers our heart so that we can clearly see that Jesus fully and eternally reflects

Left: Damascus road

MATSON PHOTO COLLECTION/ LIBRARY OF CONGRESS

Suffering Saints

No doubt each of the following servants had moments of glory, but in the end they all suffered greatly for the gospel. Read the following verses and fill in the blanks to discover the travails suffered by some of Jesus' followers.

When Herod heard of it, he said, "John, the one I ___________ has been raised!" (Mark 6:16).

They were ___________ Stephen as he called out: "Lord Jesus, receive my spirit!" (Acts 7:59).

About that time King Herod cruelly ___________ some who belonged to the church, and he ___________ ___________ John's brother, with the ___________ (Acts 12:1-2).

When he saw that it pleased the Jews, he proceeded to ___________ Peter too, during the days of Unleavened Bread. After the arrest, he _____ _____ ___ ___________ and assigned four squads of four soldiers each to guard him, intending to bring him out to the people after the Passover (Acts 12:3-4).

List any personal sufferings on behalf of Christ. How do they compare to the early disciples? Would you say they're worth it?

God's glory. His was no temporary or fading glory! It is our experience of this truth that compels us to serve Him by serving others.

Personal Reflection

1. All believers will experience doubts about their incompetence for ministry. How should we handle these feelings of insufficiency?

2. What are the biblical and social factors that keep us from expressing boldness in our ministry? How do we overcome them?

3. How does transformation from glory to glory occur? Take into account Romans 12:1-2.

4. Are you ever guilty of drawing attention to your hard work for Christ or are you offended when no one thanks you for your hard work? How do we handle such feelings?

A CLOSER LOOK

The Call

We often artificially separate the call to conversion and the call to ministry. Read Paul's testimony in Acts 26:12-23 and you will notice that the two are inextricably bound together. Jesus commands the stricken Paul to get up on his feet, "For I have appeared to you for this very purpose, to appoint you as a servant and a witness of what you have seen" (v. 16). In Galatians, speaking of his conversion, Paul writes that God had called him by His grace and had chosen to reveal "His Son in me, so that I could preach Him among the Gentiles" (1:15-16). "Ministry" and "witness" is who we are before it is what we do. Our most effective witness is the revelation of God's Son in us.

1. F. F. Bruce, *The New Century Bible Commentary: I & 2 Corinthians* (Grand Rapids: Eerdmans, 1971), 188.

2. R. V. G. Tasker, *2 Corinthians: An Introduction and a Commentary* (London: The Tyndale Press, 1958), 67.

CHAPTER THREE

The Eternal Perspective of Ministry

2 CORINTHIANS 4:7–5:10

I had just returned from England and was teaching at Wingate College. I taught an evening class which I thoroughly enjoyed because a large number of laymen from the community attended the class. Normally, the participants stayed after the course and continued the conversation about the topic we had been discussing, but not this evening. It wasn't their fault. I was preoccupied all evening, thinking about the Wake Forest basketball game I was missing on the radio. It was an important game; tournament seeding was on the line. I actually dismissed class early and sprinted to our small faculty apartment.

When I arrived at the apartment, I was disturbed to see that several faculty wives were still there. *Why were they still hanging around; their meeting was over some time ago. Surely, they must be aware that a critical game was being played.* With a fleeting acknowledgment of their presence, I went to the radio and turned it on and tuned to the game. It was the last quarter and the score went back and forth. Wake lost in the last minute due to a terrible call, which, of course, was my own interpretation since I could not actually see the game.

Fuming, I turned the radio off and stomped into the bedroom where Paula was already in bed. If I was expecting any sympathy from my wife, I was sorely mistaken. She rolled over, and looking me in the eyes, addressed my rude behavior when I had walked into the home and took over the living room, barely acknowledging our guests. I was preparing my defense based on the importance of the game when she concluded with an undeniable truth. "If you had half as much concern for the lost students on this campus as you do for the score of a basketball game, there would be few lost students left!" OUCH! She was right. Why was I so passionate about something that had no eternal significance and so passive about those things which impact eternity?

When we view our daily lives from an eternal perspective, our priorities are greatly altered. Paul spoke about his ministry from the viewpoint of heaven. He focused on the unseen rather than the seen; the eternal rather than the temporary.

When we view our daily lives from an eternal perspective, our priorities are greatly altered.

An Eternal Treasure in an Earthen Vessel (2 Cor. 4:7-9)

The container usually will provide a reliable clue to what is inside. For example, an expensive ring is usually placed in a box of fitting dignity and beauty. In the case of our ministry, we have a priceless treasure in a simple earthen vessel. Verse 7 is clearly linked to the discussion of the glory of God in the face of Christ from verse 6. To know the glory of God in the face of Christ is the most treasured possession we can know and to make that glory known to others is our greatest privilege. This priceless treasure has been entrusted to men and women, simple clay vessels.

The contrast could not be more striking. The treasure is indestructible and indescribable, yet it has been placed in a fragile and very ordinary clay vessel. **Clay jars** refers to the inexpensive earthenware containers that could be bought for a penny or two in the market place. It is like someone placed a priceless jewel in an earthenware jar. We recently visited London with our grandkids and we stood in line with all the other tourists to visit the crown jewels. The display cases for these priceless jewels were impressive and expensive. What a mystery to ponder—God put the priceless gospel in the care of a human vessel subject to limitations and infirmities.

We might wonder why God would choose such a seemingly worthless vessel for His precious message. The answer—**So that this extraordinary power may be from God and not from us.** The priceless treasure in a fragile vessel is but

Below: First century oil lamp made of clay

ILLUSTRATOR PHOTO/ BOB SCHATZ/ DEPT. OF ANTIQUITIES IN JORDAN ARCHAEOLOGICAL MUSEUM/ AMMAN (8/22/2)

one demonstration of the divine law that God's strength is made perfect in human weakness (see 12:9). The contrast between the contents and the container makes it clear that the gospel and its powerful presentation is not a product of human intellect or cleverness, but a revelation of the power of God. This singular truth should give us great confidence as we share the gospel in the power of the Holy Spirit.

Paul continued the theme of fragile vessel in the next two verses with a series of four participles which contrast the daily challenges which often emerge from ministry with the divine power which works to redeem such circumstances. The redemption of our human weaknesses makes them a platform for the manifestation of God's glory.

The idea behind the phrase, **pressured in every way but not crushed** may have come from the world of sport where a combatant gives his opponent little room for action, but is unable to make him to surrender. **Perplexed but not in despair** emphasizes the limited human provision which may be confusing, at times, but never leads to despair. **Persecuted but not abandoned** speaks to a hunted man who is aware that he has not been left to his own resources. When the minister of the gospel is **struck down** he is not **destroyed.** No one said that ministry would be easy. However, it will always be victorious when we have an eternal focus.

No one said that ministry would be easy. However, it will always be victorious when we have an eternal focus.

An Eternal Perspective for Daily Living (2 Cor. 4:10-15)

The fourfold mention of **Jesus** in verses 10-11 demonstrates how Paul constantly kept in mind the earthly ministry of the Lord. Since a servant is not greater than his master, we should not be surprised when we encounter challenges similar to our Lord.

The word translated **death** in verse 10 would be better translated as "dying." Paul was not identifying with the death of Christ, but with His daily exposure to danger and death. Jesus was constantly attacked by his opponents, He was rejected by His own people, and He described His itinerant ministry with terms related to homelessness. It has been said that Jesus' death on the cross was but the final stage of "dying" that was the earthly journey of the Suffering Servant. For Paul, present-day sufferings which were the result of ministry were to be embraced as a part of one's daily death to self. "I affirm by the pride in you that I have in Christ Jesus our Lord: I die every day!" (1 Cor. 15:31).

Paul made it clear that bearing in our body the "dying" of Jesus is more than symbolic language; it is the basis for earthly ministry. The minister must die to self in order to live to and for Christ. Such dying to self will prepare one to suffer emotionally, mentally, or physically for His sake when called on to do so. It is instructive to read Paul's description of the lot of first century apostles as recorded in 1 Corinthians 4:9-13. He spoke of men condemned to die, fools for Christ sake, dishonored, hungry, thirsty, poorly clothed, roughly treated, homeless, reviled, persecuted, slandered, the world's garbage.

The fact that earthly suffering and ill-treatment did not overwhelm Paul was but one more indication that the life of Jesus was being manifest in his mortal flesh. The victorious response to such earthly treatment simply provided God a platform to reveal the life of Jesus in the mortal flesh of another clay jar. While the fragility of flesh was an experience of daily human existence, the life-giving Spirit was for Paul a guarantee that he would share in the resurrection life of Christ.

Paul gladly embraced his share of earthly sufferings because his ministry meant life for others—**So death works in us, but life in you.** Because Paul's sufferings gave clear evidence of the power of the risen Christ, they were a source of life to the recipients of his ministry. In this case, the Corinthian believers had been the recipients of Paul's willingness to carry about in his body the "dying" of Christ.

But even if Paul had been unable to celebrate in the wonderful benefits brought about by his suffering, he would still not be discouraged nor would he abandon his ministry. Paul accepted the language of the psalmist—**"I believed, therefore I spoke"** as his own testimony (see Ps. 116:10). Believers are compelled by faith—even when circumstances turn against us and we have little visible earthly evidence to the contrary—to declare our faith. Paul's faith was based on an irrefutable certainty—**We know that the One who raised the Lord Jesus will raise us also with Jesus and present us with you.**

Left: Bronze statuette of a wrestler lifting an opponent off the ground; Hellenistic period (2nd-1st century B.C.)

ILLUSTRATOR PHOTO/ BRENT BRUCE/ WALTERS ART MUSEUM/ BALTIMORE (75/0154)

According to his own testimony, Paul frequently had been delivered from what appeared to be certain death, but he knew that one day death would come for him as it does for all mankind. He was undeterred by this knowledge because he was convinced that God who raised Jesus would raise Paul along with the Corinthian believers. **Raise us also with Jesus** speaks to the believers union with Christ. All who are in Christ remain in Christ whether they are alive or dead. His resurrection is the guarantee of our resurrection. It is this truth that provides motivation for ministry and hope for the future.

Paul's contemplation of the eternal communion of all saints (**present us with you**) leads to the affirmation—**everything is for your benefit.** Paul could not think of his eternal blessings apart from that of his people. All of his ministry and its accompanying suffering had, as its ultimate objective, the eternal welfare of his converts. Thus, he affirmed that the more people who come to know the grace of God through the preaching of the gospel, the more abundant will be the thanksgivings that overflow to God's glory. Unlike some of his opponents, Paul wanted glory to go to God and not to himself.

An Eternal Focus Gives Victory over Affliction (2 Cor. 4:16-18)

I love the victorious note sounded by Paul in verse 16—**Therefore we do not give up.** This is the second time he affirmed it in this chapter (4:1). Anyone who has ever been engaged in ministry has been tempted at one time or another to give up. With all the challenges Paul faced, what could give him such resolve? He was confident that even though the physical challenges of life and ministry meant the **outer person is being destroyed, our inner person is being renewed day by day.**

Outer person is a comprehensive expression that includes everything implied in the terms *clay jars* (v. 7), *body* (v. 10), and *mortal flesh* (v. 11). This outer person is subject to the ravages of age and the physical challenges presented by ministry. While the outer person is being destroyed, our inner person is experiencing daily renewal. For Paul, the inner person is the highest part of our being where the Holy Spirit brings new life and daily renewal. As our physical facilities fail, the things of the Spirit become even more vital. Paul prayed for the Ephesian believers—"I pray that He may grant you, according to the riches of His glory to be strengthened with power in the inner man through His Spirit" (3:16).

When we read the list of Paul's sufferings in 2 Corinthians 11:22-28, we are impressed that he could refer to them as a **momentary light affliction.** Shipwrecks; beatings; dangers on every side; and a lack of sleep, food, and clothing are not normally classified as monetary light affliction. But they are nothing when compared with the **absolutely incomparable eternal weight of glory** they are producing. It is not simply that glory will compensate us for our suffering; glory is the product of affliction. All our earthly afflictions are of relatively short duration

Keys to Renewal

Read the passages below to discover the keys to renewal.

Isaiah 40:31: ______________ in the Lord = renewed strength

Psalm 19:7: __________________ of the Lord = renewed life

Psalm 51:10: ______________ heart = renewed spirit

Psalm 103:5: Satisfied with ______________ = renewed youth

Romans 12:2: Nonconformance to this ________ = renewed mind

Answers:
Trust in the Lord = renewed strength
Instruction of the Lord = renewed life
Clean heart = renewed spirit
Satisfied with goodness = renewed youth
Nonconformance to this age = renewed mind

and thus when viewed in the light of eternal glory are inconsequential. Eternity is so eternal and glory is so glorious that all earthly afflictions are so mundane.

Eternity is so eternal and glory is so glorious that all earthly afflictions are so mundane.

When Peter declared that the disciples had left everything to follow Him, Jesus spoke of His glorious exaltation and reign. He declared, "And everyone who has left houses, brothers or sister, father or mother, children, or fields because of My name will receive 100 times and will inherit eternal life" (Matt. 19:29). Paul encouraged young Timothy with a trustworthy saying, "For if we have died with Him, we will also live with Him; if we endure, we will also reign with Him" (2 Tim. 2:11-12).

Focus determines the direction or trajectory of one's life. When I was small, I loved to plow the garden with my dad. He would plow it with a pair of mules he borrowed from a neighbor. I was amazed by how straight a row my dad could plow. When I asked him how he could plow such a straight row with such ornery mules, he told me he always picked an object at the end of the garden and steered the mule straight at that object.

Paul chose to focus on the **unseen** and the **eternal** rather than the **seen** and **temporary.** In his ministry, Paul chose not to dwell on the difficulties and troubles he encountered—the seen and the temporary—but to keep his focus on the things that God has prepared for those who love him. Paul made this same point in his first letter, quoting from Isaiah 52:15 and 64:4—"What eye did not see and ear did not hear, and what never entered the human mind—God prepared this for those who love Him" (1 Cor. 2:9). Do you sometimes find that you get so focused on daily challenges that you lose sight of God's calling and purpose for your life?

Heaven or Earth?

Focusing on what is eternal rather than temporal takes prayer, prioritizing, and practice. From each pair below, choose the response that you believe skews more eternal than temporal and circle it:

assuming you will live forever — assuming your life is fleeting
public worship — private worship
beauty and charm — fear of the Lord
worship service — sporting event
material possessions — treasure in heaven
building a house — building up a church
idle talk — prayer
physical exercise — godliness
spending time with family — spending time in the workplace
encouraging a friend — working late
college degree — Bible study
staying late at the office — eating dinner with the family
earning a living — parenting children
marriage — career

Are you down to earth or heavenly minded? Put a x to indicate where you believe your focus is.

Temporal Eternal

An Assured Eternity Creates Confidence (2 Cor. 5:1-8)

This passage begins and ends with a note of profound confidence. **For we know** indicates the issue being discussed is a certainty that transforms all earthly groaning (vv. 2,4) into overcoming confidence (vv. 6,8). Paul continued to address the issue of human frailty by contrasting the human body to the heavenly one we will one day inhabit.

The human body is a **temporary, earthly dwelling,** or a **tent,** in contrast to **an eternal dwelling in the heavens, not made with hands.** It is a temporary dwelling because its purpose is to shelter us and provide a platform for ministry during the few years of our earthly pilgrimage. Since it is a tent, it is vulnerable to the wear and tear of everyday life. Someday the tent will be destroyed by death unless one lives until the Lord returns.

A CLOSER LOOK
The earthly tent (2 Cor. 5:4)

The folding of the earthly tent! While I was writing this section, I received a call from my sister telling me that her husband was in hospice care and had only a short time to live. Bill had been staging a heroic but losing battle with cancer. Dot had been his caretaker for years and it was painful for her to watch as the cancer began to shred the canvas of his earthly tent. Bill had been an avid golfer and possessed an indomitable sense of humor. First the physical body began to deteriorate and his constant weight loss became obvious to all who visited. His walking became more difficult and the periods that he could venture from his bed and his home became shorter and less frequent. When I walked into the facility, the shell that occupied the bed bore little resemblance to the man with whom I had enjoyed a spirited round of golf. His breathing was labored, his skin was pale, and the tent material was stretched tight over the framework of the tent. It was painful for

family and friends to watch the folding of the earthly tent, but glorious to celebrate the truth that Bill had a new home, not made with hands already reserved for him in the heavens. I was privileged to share from this passage that had been my constant companion for days. Isn't God good!

But we are not reduced to despair by the destruction of the earthly tent since we know that **we have a building from God.** Paul indicated that our eternal dwelling already exists in the heavens. This causes us to remember the promise Jesus gave to His first disciples to comfort them concerning His imminent death. "Your heart must not be troubled. Believe in God; believe also in Me. In My Father's house are many dwelling places; if not, I would have told you. I am going away to prepare a

Left: Interior of a bedouin tent. Paul was a tentmaker by trade (Acts 18:3).

ILLUSTRATOR PHOTO/ MIKE RUTHERFORD (59/1111)

place for you" (John 14:2). The designer and builder of our eternal dwelling is God. When we contrast an earthly tent with a dwelling fashioned by God, groaning turns into rejoicing.

When we contrast an earthly tent with a dwelling fashioned by God, groaning turns into rejoicing.

Paul changed from the image of a house to that of a garment that will be put on. Groaning in this body can refer both to the pain of present affliction experienced in our fragile earthly tent, and also to the growing desire to enjoy the heavenly garment that awaits us. We groan because of the pain we experience in the dismantling of the tent and we groan because we desire our glorious tent.

It is possible that Paul was also saying he would prefer to put on his new body over his present body, as will be the case when the Lord returns. In that case, he was groaning for this new dwelling before the old tent was taken down through death. In 1 Corinthians 15 Paul spoke of the transformation of both the living and the dead at the return of the Lord:

> Listen! I am telling you a mystery: we will not all fall asleep, but we will all be changed, in a moment, in the blink of an eye, at the last trumpet. For the trumpet will sound, and the dead will be raised incorruptible, and we will be changed (1 Cor. 15:51-52).

Verse 3 is a like a parenthesis that explains why we long to put on our heavenly dwelling—**since, when we are clothed, we will not be found naked.** This verse raises questions as to whether Paul envisioned a time when those who died prior to the return of the Lord would be "naked" in the sense that they would be awaiting the incorruptible body they would receive at the resurrection. Paul did not give us sufficient detail to answer that question with any certainty. He did, however, affirm with great conviction that a heavenly shelter awaited him after death and this certainty was in no way diminished by the thought that his departure to be with Christ may precede the Lord's return in glory and his own assumption of the resurrection body.[1] Could it be that in the consciousness of the departed there is no interval between the taking off of the earthly tent and the putting on of the house built by God no matter how much time may have passed in terms of earthly years?

Paul again returned to the groaning created by the burdens of our existence in the present temporary tent we inhabit. We should not see Paul's desire to put on his new tent as a morbid wish for death because of the frailties of the present body; rather it was a passionate desire to enjoy the protection of an imperishable and permanent heavenly shelter. He looked with anticipation to the time when human mortality is **swallowed up by life.**

This is not simply wishful thinking to help one cope with the trials of earthly existence. God has **prepared us for this very purpose.** Man was created in God's image to enjoy His presence and serve Him eternally. We need only to think of Adam's existence in the garden before the fall. Sin intervened and with it came separation from God and physical death. The penalty of sin has been paid by Christ and now those in Christ have been redeemed and prepared for an eternal dwelling with God. In fact, we have received the down payment of life eternal—the Holy Spirit, who now indwells and empowers us. The gift of the Spirit is God's assurance that one day we will be clothed with immortality. We can actually see the process of eternal life at work in us as the Holy Spirit daily conforms us from glory into glory (3:18), preparing us for the day we receive our heavenly body.

In verses 6-8 Paul twice affirmed his absolute confidence in the Lord whether he remained alive in the physical body or out of his earthly tent and at home with the Lord. We learn from Paul that confidence in the faithfulness of the Lord and the reality of those things presently unseen enables us to face difficulties with a sure hope. If earthly circumstances overwhelm us with despair, it is a negation of the work of the Spirit in our lives, who is the assurance of the present and future work of Christ.

Confidence in the faithfulness of the Lord and the reality of those things presently unseen enables us to face difficulties with a sure hope.

While we are in the body and away from the Lord, we must **walk by faith, not by sight.** *Walk* means the ordering or conduct of one's life. Thus our earthly existence is characterized by faith. Our being **away from the Lord** is not to be understood in an absolute sense, since God is everywhere, but must be understood in terms of our face to face communion. Our present communion with God must be maintained by faith and not by sight. It is a faith that is based on unwavering confidence in the absolute certainty of God's Word. Paul wrote in Romans 10:17, "So faith comes from what is heard, and what is heard comes through the message about Christ." If your faith is weak, it can be strengthened by hearing and acting on God's Word.

An Eternal Focus Creates Clear Life Purpose (2 Cor. 5:9-10)

What then should be the end result of our confidence in the certainty of our eternal home in the presence of the Lord? Paul declared that we should **make it our aim to be pleasing to Him.** Our earthly ambition—the compelling passion of life—is to please our Creator and Redeemer. For the believer, there will always be a tension between our desire to live productively on earth and to enjoy the unhindered presence of our Lord.

In Philippians 1:21-24, Paul expressed this tension between productive earthly ministry and the natural longing for his heavenly home. As you read it, notice again his absolute certainty of his future destiny.

> For me, living is Christ and dying is gain. Now if I live on in the flesh, this means fruitful work for me; and I don't know which one I should choose. I am pressured by both. I have the desire to depart and be with Christ—which is far better—but to remain in the flesh is more necessary for you.

Death will not only enable the believer to be present with Christ, it also will bring us nearer the day that we will appear before the judgment seat of Christ and be repaid for what we have done in the body; what we have done with the gifts—time, talents, treasures, and opportunities God has given us on earth. The thought of judgment has great solemnity. It should not frighten us about our eternal destiny but motivate us concerning our earthly ministry. It should cause us to live daily with the passion to be pleasing to the Lord.

There are some persons who seem to think that there is an inconsistency between the doctrine of justification by faith alone and a final judgment for our actions and works, but such is not the case. Already in 1 Corinthians 3:12-15 Paul had declared that the quality of each believers work will be tested by fire. Work that survives the testing of fire will provide a reward, while that which is burned up will be lost. Paul quickly reminded them that the loss of reward does not mean that the individual will be lost. True believers cannot lose their salvation, but they can lose the privilege of serving God with their totality of their earthly lives. Paul continued the theme of the judgment of believers in 1 Corinthians 4:1-5. He declared that one day he would be evaluated by the Lord, who will bring to light things hidden in darkness and the intention of the heart. I love the concluding affirmation of this section—"And then praise will come to each one from God" (1 Cor. 4:5).

The reality of the judgment for our works means that our ministry is so important to God that He holds us accountable.

The thought of the judgment seat of Christ should not bring fear but proper motivation for ministry. The reality of the judgment for our works means that our ministry is so important to God that He holds us accountable. Thus we are not surprised that Paul would preach justification by faith alone to unbelievers and divine judgment for works for every believer. This is a wonderful doctrine that affirms us as gifted members of Christ's body.

Personal Reflection

1. How would your life change if you approached each day and each event with an eternal perspective?

2. How knowing that God has put His priceless treasure in your "earthen vessel" motivate you? How can you make the treasure inside more visible to others?

3. Do you ever find yourself complaining about life being "unfair" when you are treated badly or called on to suffer? What encouragement do you find from 2 Corinthians 4:7–5:10?

4. Does the idea of the judgment seat of Christ frighten or motivate you? How does this idea change your thinking about ministry?

1. R.V.G. Tasker, *2 Corinthians: An Introduction and Commentary* (London: The Tyndale Press, 1958), 80.

CHAPTER FOUR

The Gospel Focus of Ministry

2 CORINTHIANS 5:11–7:16

My dad was my pastor and therefore very few meetings of the church were optional for me when I was a young boy. One meeting that was a favorite of mine was our Royal Ambassador meeting. The "RA's," as we called them, was an organization for young men. Most meetings were preceded by some sports activity and since I loved all sports, I couldn't wait for the night for our RA meeting to roll around each week.

While I was initially drawn to the meeting by the prospect of a rough and tumble game of tackle football, usually without pads, I actually enjoyed the meeting time. Through certain learning activities we could earn patches that could be sown to your shirt or hat. Each meeting began with a pledge that affirmed that a Royal Ambassador is one who represents the person of the King at the court of another. While I may not have fully understood what that pledge meant, I do remember being impressed that God wanted to use me to represent him on earth. That idea profoundly impacted me then and continues to do so until this very day.

In this chapter we are going to look at the context of the passage which declares those who have been reconciled to God have, in turn, been given the ministry of reconciliation and serve as royal ambassadors. This truth affirms that the foundation and focus of ministry is the gospel of Jesus Christ. Ministry is grounded in the overwhelming affirmation that God was in Christ reconciling the world to Himself. Being an ambassador for Christ means that we have the privilege of cooperating with God in the reconciling of all peoples to Him, their rightful King.

Love: The Compelling Force of Ministry (2 Cor. 5:11-15)

In the previous chapter we ended with the sobering truth that we will all appear before the judgment seat of Christ to be rewarded for what we have accomplished in this body. Paul continued, **Therefore, because we know the fear of the Lord, we seek to persuade people.** The *fear of the Lord* is not a cringing fear, but a sense of awe and reverence which is appropriate to one who knows and loves the Lord and will one day stand before Him in judgment. It was the eternal focus of his ministry that kept Paul focused despite the difficulties he continually faced.

Paul saw his primary work in ministry as persuading others of the truth of the gospel. The verb *persuade* here is in the present tense and thus indicates that persuading others was a continuing focus of his entire ministry. If one truly comprehends the truth that God has reconciled sinful man to Himself through Christ, no message has greater relevance or importance. For that reason, the gospel was the compelling force for Paul's ministry and should be for ours.

Having spoken to that which compelled him, Paul once again affirmed his complete openness and integrity in ministry. He wanted to be as transparent before the Corinthians as he was before God who would judge his every thought and motive. The fact that he would one day stand before God gave him the courage to be completely open before the Corinthians. The awareness that God alone is our ultimate judge will help us to avoid the desire to please everyone and also desensitizes us to the pain of unjust criticism.

The awareness that God alone is our ultimate judge will help us to avoid the desire to please everyone.

Paul wanted the Corinthian believers to understand that he was not interested in commending himself, a point he made earlier in 3:1. However, Paul knew that he had serious detractors in Corinth and that their accusations had an impact on the community. His motive in defending his ministry was to provide the Corinthian believers with the ammunition they needed to reply to those who were attempting to discredit Paul's work. Paul described his opponents as men **who take pride in the outward appearance rather than in the heart.** This is essentially the same critique found in 11:18, where he spoke of those who boast from a human perspective. His opponents boasted in their grand visions and powerful revelations, whereas Paul boasted in his pure motives and clear conscience.

It is possible that some of Paul's critics had suggested that he was mad (v. 13). Perhaps when he spoke to them with real

spiritual emotion he may have appeared to be beside himself. It is also possible that the phrase ***out of our mind*** in verse 13 could be a reference to ecstatic experiences and visions. We know from 1 Corinthians that some in Corinth were focused on the more visible and audible of the spiritual gifts and likely claimed that such gifts proved their advanced spirituality. From 2 Corinthians 12 it is apparent that some of Paul's opponents boasted in their visions and may have based their message on a revelation given in a vision. In response, Paul spoke about his own visionary experience only to conclude that what he heard was inexpressible and thus led him to boast in his own weakness, not to glory in the experience (12:1-5). If

Left: The Rostra (Bema) at Corinth dates from the middle of the first century A.D. It is thought to be the Bema mentioned in the Book of Acts. The Apostle Paul was brought to the Bema by the elders of Corinth's synagogue, who accused him of subversive teaching against the mosaic law. The proconsul Gallio, however, judged that the teaching did not constitute an offence against the Roman law.

ILLUSTRATOR PHOTO/ GB HOWELL (35/30/57)

that is what is in mind here, Paul was saying that any ecstatic experience is between the person and the Lord and should never lead to self-glorification. Being of **sound mind** then would carry the same emphasis as the admonition to pray and sing with understanding in 1 Corinthians 14:15. When Paul was ministering to the church, he wanted his words and actions to be clearly understood (see 1 Cor. 14:19).

If Paul was not interested in the applause of men or the thrill of ecstasy, what is it that compelled him to give his life in ministry? Simply but powerfully stated, he was compelled by Christ's love—Christ's love for man, Christ's love for Paul. This love was so overwhelming that Paul had no choice but to serve Him by serving others. That love, experienced on the Damascus road, had transformed his life and griped his heart with such force he saw no other option except a life of service to the one who died for all.

The dramatic conclusion that changed the trajectory of Paul's life was this: **If One died for all, then all died.** Christ's death was unlimited in its inclusiveness—One died for all. His death was representative of the death of all mankind in the sense that He died the death that all should have died. The penalty of sin was death or eternal separation from God. The penalty of death was borne by Christ. The only One undeserving of death died in the place of sinful mankind. Paul was not speaking theoretically, he saw himself among those deserving death.

Those who have died with Christ and have been raised with Him can no longer live for themselves.

The implication of such a sacrificial death on behalf of sinful mankind is clear—**He died for all so that those who live should no longer live for themselves, but for the One who died for them and was raised.** The unlimited death created the possibility of unlimited atonement for all who would receive it. Those who have died with Christ and have been raised with Him can no longer live for themselves. The old man is dead and thus has no claim over our affections or our lives. Death to self gives birth to a new life which is centered on the One who died for us and gave us resurrection life.

Reconciliation: The Ministry of the Ambassador (2 Cor. 5:16-21)

Life as a new creation brings with it different standards of evaluation. Before his conversion, Paul had a view of life that was based on purely human evaluation and thus led to wrong conceptions about the Messiah and about men. Like many Jews of his day, Paul was looking for a powerful political Messianic conqueror who would free the Jews from foreign domination. He had concluded that one who was born in obscurity, who taught and behaved with such kindness to Jew and Gentile alike, and who died such a humiliating death could not be the long-awaited Messiah. Therefore, he had dismissed Jesus as a blasphemer and persecuted all who claimed to be His followers.

After Paul's encounter with the risen Lord on the Damascus road, his understanding of Jesus and his fellow man were both radically altered. He no longer viewed Christ in a purely human way. He now knew Him to be the risen Christ and his personal Savior and Lord. But there is more! Paul declared that he no longer knew **anyone in a purely human way.** His disdain for the hated Gentiles was now replaced with a love that compelled him to attempt to persuade them of the truth of the gospel. Do you now see your friends, neighbors, and even past enemies as people who need to be persuaded of the truth of the gospel? Has your own conversion caused a radical change in your world view?

The total transformation of one's worldview is a sign of the transformation that takes place in the person who is in Christ.

The total transformation of one's worldview is a sign of the transformation that takes place in the person who is in Christ. The person in Christ has already crossed the bridge from the old to the new and fully anticipates that one day only the new will survive. The new things foretold by Isaiah have become a reality. "Do not remember the past events, pay no attention to things of old" (43:18; see also 65:17). Each person regenerated by Christ has experienced the new birth and thus is **a new creation.** When we fully comprehend the radical disconnect we have with the old, we will cease to use our old character traits and behavior patterns as an excuse for our lack of obedience and service.

Everything is from God means that the entire new order is the handiwork of God in the same sense that the original creation was wrought by Him. God took the initiative in reconciling sinful man to Himself. God had enabled the reconciliation by Christ's death on the cross. Man in his fallen state was an enemy of God and banished from His holy presence, but God stepped out of heaven and paid the high price of reconciliation by giving His own Son as the ransom payment for sinful man. It is for this reason that God no longer was **counting their trespasses against them.** Christ had paid the penalty required by our trespasses.

This truth, almost too wonderful to explain or to comprehend, must be preached and accepted by sinful man and for that reason God calls those **reconciled** to **the ministry of reconciliation** (v. 18). He has not only given us the ministry of reconciliation but he has committed to us **the message of reconciliation—in Christ, God was reconciling the world to Himself, not counting their trespasses against them.**

This message is not applicable to one period of history or one group of people but it is for the world and for all time until the Lord returns. It is universal in its scope and unlimited in its efficacy. It must be proclaimed to the entire world and to every man and woman since all have sinned and stand under God's righteous judgment. The only ones who can proclaim this message with integrity and conviction are those who have already been reconciled to God. This ministry of reconciliation continues and followers of Christ are now given the privilege of cooperating with God in this kingdom activity.

The logical conclusion is now clearly stated—**Therefore, we are ambassadors for Christ.** An ambassador is a messenger or representative of another. The ambassador does not speak on his own initiative or based on his own authority. He is under orders to speak in the name and authority of another. He does not communicate his own opinion or give his own conditions for peace; he simply declares the terms of the treaty as given to him by the one who commissioned him. The ambassador for Christ can speak with the certainty that **God is appealing through us.** In response to his commission, Paul made an impassioned appeal to all who are at enmity with God—**We plead on Christ's behalf, "Be reconciled to God."**

We do not have to compose our own message nor do we have to deliver it in our own power.

The use of the plural *we* leads us to conclude that Paul was not the only nor the last of those called to be an ambassador. It is the calling for each one of each generation who has been reconciled to God. It is both commission and privilege. This passage should provide both impetus and encouragement for our ministry of reconciliation. We do not have to compose our own message nor do we have to deliver it in our own power. The message is profoundly simple—**In Christ, God was reconciling the world to Himself, not counting their trespasses against them.** The power is beyond comprehension—**God is appealing through us.**

Paul concluded this section with a further explanation of the miracle of the reconciliation of sinful man to holy God. The sinless One was made sin by being condemned to a criminal's death so that those who stood condemned by their own sin might be acquitted by a holy God enabling them to become the **righteousness of God in Him.** Christ became our sin offering so that at the moment of His death He offered His life to God as an atonement for man's sin (see Rom. 8:3). F.F. Bruce wrote, "Paul has chosen this exceptional wording in order to emphasize the 'sweet exchange' whereby sinners are given a righteous status before God through the righteous one who absorbed their sin (and its judgment) in himself."[1]

Every Believing Man's Mandate

Read these passages and summarize the ministry that Christ has called every believer to perform.

Acts 1:8

James 5:16

Hebrews 13:2

Matthew 28:19-20

John 13:34

Proverbs 14:31

Ephesians 2:10

Answers:
Acts 1:8—Witnessing; James 5:16—Intercessory Prayer; Hebrews 13:2—Hospitality; Matthew 28:19-20—Making disciples; John 13:34—Love; Proverbs 14:31—Giving to poor; Ephesians 2:10—Good works

Cooperation with God: The Mystery of Ministry (2 Cor. 6:1-13)

I think many believers are reluctant to get involved in ministry because they don't see themselves as competent or worthy to be effective workers in the spiritual realm. Paul began chapter 6 with an interesting observation about his own ministry which applies to all believers. **Working together with Him** indicates that all ministry is simply a cooperation with God in His work. Paul had already articulated this truth in the first letter to the Corinthians—"For we are God's coworkers. You are God's field, God's building" (3:9).

Many believers are reluctant to get involved in ministry because they don't see themselves as competent or worthy.

As a co-worker with God, Paul appealed to the Corinthians not to **receive God's grace in vain.** The message of God's grace is at the heart of the gospel and must be appropriated by faith. Anyone who harbors the smallest vestige of hope that they can be made right with God through human achievement would be guilty of receiving God's grace in vain. The gospel is not simply good news, it is urgent news. Paul thus fortified his appeal with a quotation from Isaiah 49:8. In the original context it is a message from Yahweh to His Servant, commissioning Him to release the captives and restore the exiles. Further, it indicates a time when salvation would be offered to the Gentiles. The Corinthians were living in **the acceptable time** and thus they must accept or reject the invitation extended by God. Implicit in this verse is the truth that the acceptable time will one day expire.

The gospel is not simply good news, it is urgent news.

With so much at stake in Paul's ministry and message he turned once again to a defense of his ministry so that no possibility would exist that someone might stumble based on the accusations being hurled against their founder. It was true then and it is true now that people who are looking for an excuse to ignore the gospel will attempt to find such an excuse in the conduct of its ministers. For his part, Paul would do everything possible to ensure that his ministry was not blamed (v. 3).

In verses 4-5, Paul listed nine different kinds of trials, arranged in three groups of three, which stood as the commendation of his ministry. The list begins with **endurance**, which is the key to faithful ministry in difficult circumstances. The first group of trials—**afflictions, hardship,** and **difficulties**—are somewhat general in nature. The second grouping—**beatings, imprisonments,** and **riots** speak to specific events in the life and ministry of Paul. You might find it helpful to read the more detailed list provided in 2 Corinthians 11:23-27. The third group—**labors, sleepless nights,** and **times of hunger**—are specific in nature and are repeated in chapter 11. Paul labored as a bi-vocational minister so as not to cause anyone to stumble. Such a rigorous schedule led to sleepless nights and a lack of adequate provision.

Paul next enumerated the spiritual graces that made it possible for him to bear up under such great trial. He spoke of moral **purity, knowledge, patience,** and **kindness**, all empowered **by the Holy Spirit.** His motivation came from a **sincere love** and his **message** was revealed **truth** from God that was based on the **power of God** (see 1 Cor. 2:2-5). The **weapons of righteousness** remind us of the armor of God that Paul would write about in the Ephesian letter. The **right hand and the left** speak to weapons that are both offensive and defensive—the sword in the right hand and the shield in the left.

In his ministry, Paul received honor from some and was treated with no respect by others (v. 8; see also 1 Cor. 4:6-13). He had been criticized and flattered. He has been accused of falsehood even though he was true to the gospel. Some failed to recognize his apostolic authority because he was not one of the original apostles, yet the impact of his ministry was well known. To some he appeared to be a dying man—possibly a reference to his constant exposure to danger. Yet when it seemed he was finished, he received new strength and vitality from the Lord. He received any and all chastening as a gift from the Lord and not a sign of His displeasure.

There were moments in his ministry that caused the great apostle to grieve, but he was **always rejoicing.** His joy, a theme he would return to momentarily, was an abiding one which revealed itself even in days of deep sorrow. In terms of the world's standards, he was **poor** and yet his ministry made many rich in terms of true riches as heirs of the kingdom of God. He described himself as one who had nothing and yet possessed everything. This affirmation reminds us of Paul's testimony recorded in Philippians chapter 3, where he declared that he joyfully counted everything as loss for the sake of Christ.

The concluding paragraph of this section is intensely personal. Paul did not often address his recipients by name, but here he declared, **We have spoken openly to you, Corinthians; our heart has been opened wide.** Paul spoke without any reserve and it has only caused him to love them all the more. The generosity of Paul's love had not been fully embraced by some in Corinth and thus they had been **limited by** their **own affections.** Paul appealed to them as **children,** imploring them to return his affection.

No one said ministry would be easy. How did reading this section impact you? The listing of afflictions and misunderstandings that accompany ministry could easily be discouraging. Yet for Paul each negative was undone by the thought of being a co-worker with God and the realization that God had turned each negative into a positive. Think through this section and allow the Spirit to apply it specifically to your life and ministry.

Balancing Act

Being separate from the world while winning the world to Christ requires painstaking balance. Mark the items below that you consider to be true ways to stay distinct from the world with a T. Place an F in front of those that you consider false. Place a question mark in front of which you're undecided. How could you come to a decision about these?

____Patronizing a retail store owned by an unbeliever
____Reading a book on the best seller list that has an anti-Christian message to discuss with an unsaved co-worker
____Marrying an unbeliever
____Playing on a softball team with believers and unbelievers
____Starting a business with your Jewish college friend
____Watching movies with Christian messages only
____Taking part in a secular book club
____Participating in politics
____Going to a bar with co-workers and drinking water while they drink alcohol
____Drinking wine at home with friends, none of whom get drunk

Growing Sanctification: The Power of Ministry (2 Cor. 6:14–7:1)

Paul's fatherly affection for the Corinthians did not keep him from giving them urgent warnings concerning the need for growing sanctification. The Corinthian church had been birthed in a city that was well-known for its immorality. One of the critical issues for any growing Christian is to know how to segregate ourselves from the sin and idolatry of people outside the Christian family and at the same time love those same persons unconditionally with the gospel.

Paul used several different images to convey the stark difference between the believer and the unbeliever. Words such as **mismatched, partnership, fellowship, agreement,** and **in common** show the absolute incompatibility of the Christian worldview and the secular world view. **Righteousness and lawlessness** have nothing in common. **Light** and **darkness** cannot co-exist since light by its very nature dispels darkness. There is no agreement between **Christ** and **Belial,** a term only used here in the New Testament for Satan. It comes from a Hebrew term meaning "worthless." Christ and Belial represent two heads of conflicting worlds and to choose one is to reject the other. For that reason the believer has nothing in common with the unbeliever. The Old Testament sanctuary was a visible symbol of God's continual presence and thus forbade all idolatry. Now the church, the body of believers in Corinth, is **the sanctuary of the living God** and thus they must avoid all compromise.

Paul linked together several Old Testament quotations to further elaborate on the truth that we are the temple of Holy God. The first reference in verse 16 is to Leviticus 26:11-12 and speaks of God's intimate presence among His people. Ezekiel uses the same language to speak of a time when God's sanctuary will be among His people forever (Ezek. 37:26). Paul preceded the second quotation with the word ***therefore,*** indicating that he was applying the truth that Christians are the temple of God. The words in verse 17 are from Isaiah 52:11 and were originally spoken by God to His people when He called them out of exile. Leaving Babylon they were to leave behind all that was unclean and take only the vessels of the Lord. Believers are separated from the world in the positive sense that they enjoy fellowship with a holy God among a holy fellowship of believers which form His new place of habitation.

Not only are believers the temple of God, they are the family of God (v. 18). Paul seemed to have had in mind God's promise to David concerning Solomon as recorded in 2 Samuel 7:14, "I will be a Father to him, and he will be a son to Me." This intimate language of a family relationship with God was also used by Jeremiah (31:9), Isaiah (43:6; 49:22; 60:4), and Hosea (1:10). This promise of intimacy with God was made by **the Lord Almighty,** the one who is all-sovereign.

Paul next applied the truth established by **such promises.** Again we should notice the intimacy and emotion in the personal address, **dear friends.** The response to these promises is stated in a negative and a corresponding positive sense. First, we should **cleanse ourselves from every impurity of the flesh and spirit.** The Christian is called to physical and spiritual purity; we are to be clean from anything that might defile. Second we are to make our **sanctification** complete as the natural response to our worship of God. The verb *completing* is a present participle which implies a continual process that has as its goal holiness, without which no man shall see God (see Heb. 12:4).

This section has sometimes been misapplied in a legalistic and negativistic sense to encourage believers to avoid any contact with the world and the sinners who inhabit it. Such a strategy would make it impossible for us to be ambassadors for Christ among those who need reconciliation to a holy God. Our separation has two parts to it—from the world and to God. We cannot be effective in reaching those who live in darkness unless we fully represent the light. We cannot reflect God's light in a world of darkness without the cleansing and purity that comes only from an intimate relationship with Him.

We cannot be effective in reaching those who live in darkness unless we fully represent the light.

Joy: The Response to Ministry Fulfilled (2 Cor. 7:2-16)

Paul addressed the concern which prompted him to write the tearful letter that had initially caused the Corinthians such pain. He explained that he did not desire for the letter to be so painful, and that immediately after writing it he had regretted sending it for he knew it might cause them pain. However, he no longer regretted the action he had taken since it produced godly sorrow which led to godly grief which led to their repentance. When you read the entire section, you will find the words *encouragement, comfort,* and *joy* repeated several times. *Joy* or *rejoice* is the predominant term (6 times) and it opens and concludes this section. When we see positive results from our ministry it brings joy.

Paul urged the Corinthians, **Accept us,** renewing the theme began in 6:13. The phrase **I have already said** in verse 3 is likely a reference to 6:11-13. They had no reason not to open their hearts to Paul since his ministry had been above reproach and had only a positive impact. Paul did not want his corrective teaching to bring any condemnation; his love for them was such that he was willing to share life and death with them (7:3). The news conveyed to him by Titus had produced in him a renewed sense of **confidence, pride, encouragement,** and **joy.**

Paul candidly spoke of his initial unrest when he had arrived in **Macedonia.** He had been afflicted by outward struggles and internal fear. **But God, who comforts the humble, comforted us by the arrival of Titus.** The safe return of Titus was itself comforting, but his message that the Corinthians had responded positively to Paul's letter with sorrow over their actions and zeal for their founder (v. 7).

The letter referred to in verses 8-13 is the "tearful" letter that had caused both distress and godly sorrow (see 2:3-4). His initial regret in having sent the letter had been replaced with joy because the Corinthians responded in genuine repentance. The pain the letter caused led to blessing. Paul contrasted **godly grief** with **worldly grief.** Godly grief was **as God willed** and resulted in **repentance** and **salvation.** Worldly grief, on the other hand, leads to **death.** It has no healing power and thus

Above: St. Titus Church at Gortyn, Crete. Titus was commissioned by the Apostle Paul to lead the first Christians on Crete (Titus 1:5).

ILLUSTRATOR PHOTO/ GB HOWELL (35/37/48)

leads to stubborn bitterness and resentment. It is not enough to be sorry for one's sin; one must experience godly sorrow which always leads to true repentance.

Paul further explained that his motivation in writing the tearful letter had never been aimed at punishing the one who did wrong nor in vindicating himself. He had written out of pure concern for them (v. 12). Paul's joy was increased because **Titus** had experienced the **joy** of effective ministry and thus had been **refreshed by** them. Paul's confidence in them and in the effective ministry of Titus had not been misplaced. As Titus had looked back on his effective ministry among the Corinthians, his **affection** for them had grown. Thus Paul could affirm—**I rejoice that I have complete confidence in you.**

Ministry is challenging and often painful but the joy created when we can celebrate the results of working together with God is reward enough.

Personal Reflection

1. What are the practical ramifications of living for the One who died for us (5:15)?

2. Knowing we are called to be ambassadors for Christ, why do we find it so challenging to share the message of reconciliation with others?

3. What first comes to mind when you think of "sanctification"? What new did you learn about sanctification from your study of 2 Corinthians 6:14–7:1?

4. Relate a recent ministry experience that caused you to rejoice.

1. F.F. Bruce, *The New Century Bible Commentary: I and II Corinthians* (Grand Rapids, Wm. B. Eerdmans, 1992), 211.

CHAPTER FIVE

The Financial Aspect of Ministry

2 CORINTHIANS 8:1–9:15

My dad was a great story-telling pastor. He loved stories that incorporated both humor and a pungent message. One Sunday when he was preaching on finances he told the story of a man who advertised a milk cow for sale. A prospective buyer asked him if the cow was a good "giver." The old farmer drawled, "Not much of a giver, but if you get her penned up, you can take a lot from her." My dad concluded that many Christians were like this when it related to stewardship. They didn't give very much from a joyful heart and had to be "penned up" by guilt-ridden appeals before you get much from them. If this has been your reaction to the matter of money and the Christian life, you should truly benefit from this chapter.

Paul was in Antioch (Acts 11:27-30) when he first heard of the famine that had ravaged the church in Jerusalem. The believers in Antioch responded immediately by sending an offering to Jerusalem by Barnabas and Saul. The great apostle to the Gentiles was so moved by the need of the Jerusalem Christians that he devoted the decade of the 50s to collecting an offering for these Jewish believers. Paul wanted not only to meet the need of fellow believers, but he wanted to demonstrate the validity of the churches that were composed primarily of Gentiles.

Corinth was one of those churches and Paul had encouraged them to support the collection for the saints in Jerusalem. He had first made this appeal in person and then had written about the need to set the money aside on the first day of the week. Their giving was to be proportionate with the resources they had been given (1 Cor. 16:1-4). Now, nearly a year later, Paul encouraged them to conclude the collection of their generous gift. In this context, he shared several timeless principles of joyous and generous giving that have encouraged Christians of every generation.

The Grace of Giving (2 Cor. 8:1-7)

A year had passed since Paul's original directions for the offering were written and a "painful letter" had been written to Corinth (2 Cor. 7:8). The response to Paul's corrective letter had been positive and so Paul now devoted two chapters to the matter of gracious giving. Take a moment to read 2 Corinthians 8:1-7 and you will find the word ***grace*** repeated three times.

The early Christian church inherited the responsibility of tithing and the giving of alms from the Jewish community. Jesus assumed that His followers would practice both (see Matt. 6:1-4 and 23:23), but He stressed the importance of avoiding ostentation and self-righteousness in giving. In other words, Jesus stressed the privilege of giving from an understanding of the graciousness of life.

Paul underlined the theme of grace as he told the Corinthians about the gracious giving of the churches of Macedonia—Philippi, Thessalonica, and Berea. This was not the first time Paul used the term *grace* in the context of giving. In his earlier instructions (1 Cor. 16:3), Paul had referred to the offering the Corinthian believers were collecting as a "gracious gift." Generosity is a visible expression of grace received. The Holy Spirit can motivate people to give generously and spontaneously to people they have never seen. The Holy Spirit can enable people to give beyond their physical means.

The Macedonian churches provided a great example of grace giving because they gave despite **a severe testing by affliction** and their **deep poverty.** It is likely that their poverty came as the direct result of the persecution. In spite of their poverty their **abundance of joy** had **overflowed into the wealth of their generosity.** Joy and generosity are twins. Joy comes from the knowledge of grace received and sins forgiven. The infinite generosity of God experienced in our redemption, when truly comprehended, will produce a life of joyful giving. Joy leads to generosity and generosity, in turn, gives one joy. Miserly people are miserable and generous people are joyous. Generosity indicates giving that is uncalculating and unpretentious, free from human motivation and pride.

Miserly people are miserable and generous people are joyous.

Paul declared that the generosity of the Macedonians was a visible expression of grace. The word *grace* actually means "generosity"—it is the generosity of God that freely gives sinners the forgiveness they don't deserve and could never afford. The use of *grace* here in relation to giving doesn't simply mean it was motivated by grace; it actually suggests that it is an act of grace. In other words it was inspired and empowered by the Holy Spirit.

If you have read 1 Corinthians, you know that the Corinthians were "zealous for spiritual gifts" (14:12). Their hunger to possess the more spectacular gifts was often motivated by the desire to be known as spiritual people. Paul attempted to redirect their spiritual zeal by encouraging them to seek those gifts that would build up the church. In our present passage, Paul was affirming that the ability to give generously **beyond their ability** was as much a demonstration of the Spirit's work as prophecy or miracle-working faith.

You may be wondering what distinguishes "grace giving" from other forms of giving. Based on the text before us, we can discern four unique characteristics of grace giving.

1. *Grace giving is spontaneous*. The phrase ***on their own*** in verse 3 indicates that no one coerced them into giving. In the light of their poverty, it is possible that Paul was reluctant to mention the offering to them. But their desire to give was so overwhelming **they begged us insistently for the privilege of sharing.** Grace givers see giving as a privilege and not a duty.

Grace givers see giving as a privilege and not a duty.

---

2. *Grace giving is beyond one's natural ability.* Paul declared that they gave **according to their ability and beyond their ability.** Grace giving enables us to move beyond proportionate giving—tithing—to supernatural giving. Many persons who argue that the tithe (10 percent) is an Old Testament legalistic requirement are often looking for an excuse to give less. Anyone who has experienced grace should desire to give beyond the tithe. Tithing could be accomplished by an Old Testament believer before the giving of the Spirit.

3. *Grace giving sees giving as a privilege of sharing in ministry.* Despite their affliction and their poverty, the Macedonian believers would not be deprived of the **privilege of sharing in the ministry to the saints.** Paul pulled together several unique words to describe the privilege of giving which are somewhat obscured by our English translation. The word translated **privilege** is the word *charis* in the Greek and is usually translated "grace." The second word is the Greek *koinonia,* (**sharing**) which is often translated "fellowship." In 1 Corinthians 1:9, Paul used *koinonia* to speak of our "fellowship with His Son." In Galatians 2:9 the same word is used to speak of fellowship between believers. In 2 Corinthians 9:13 it is translated "generosity" and in Romans 15:26 as "contribution." True fellowship flows from a relationship with the Son, it creates a bond of community, and is evidenced in our generous giving

to meet the needs of others in the family. The word translated **ministry** is from the Greek *diakonia,* from which we derive our English word *deacon*. The Macedonians saw their giving as a ministry of fellowship empowered by grace.

True fellowship flows from a relationship with the Son, it creates a bond of community, and is evidenced in our generous giving to meet the needs of others in the family.

---

4. *Grace giving begins with the giving of oneself.* The Macedonians **gave themselves especially to the Lord, then to us by God's will.** All giving stems from the offering of ourselves to the Lord as a living sacrifice (Rom. 12:1). When we have truly

Earmarks of Excellence

In 2 Corinthians 8:7 Paul identified several ways that believers are to show excellence. List them below:

1.

2.

3.

4.

5.

6.

Prayerfully grade yourself in each area: E – Excellent; S – Satisfactory; U- Unsatisfactory.

What did you base your grades on? Write an example beside each.

What can you do to improve in the areas of dissatisfaction?

Answers: 1. faith; 2. speech; 3. knowledge; 4. diligence; 5. love; 6. giving

offered ourselves to God, we will always look for opportunities of gracious service. The giving of themselves to Paul naturally followed the giving of themselves to God, since they now wanted to make themselves available to assist Paul in any way possible.

Paul was so encouraged by the generosity of the Macedonians that he urged Titus to return to Corinth **so he should also complete this grace to you.** Once again, Paul referred to the offering by the simple term *grace*. In verse 7 Paul moved beyond an appeal based on the example of the Macedonian churches to reminding the Corinthians of the spiritual riches that God had made available to them.

Verse 7 is reminiscent of 1 Corinthians 1:4-5, where Paul spoke of the abundance of their spiritual gifts—"That by Him you were enriched in everything—in all speech and all knowledge." In our present passage Paul listed faith, speech, and knowledge. Further, he mentioned their diligence and their love for him and his companions as evidence of the grace they have received and manifested. The Corinthians were proud of the abundance of their spiritual gifts, and therefore Paul used their pride in spiritual gifts to motivate them to **excel also in this grace.** It is clear that Paul saw generosity as an evidence of the grace of God and thus as a work of the Spirit.

It is clear that Paul saw generosity as an evidence of the grace of God and thus as a work of the Spirit.

Love: The Supreme Motive for Giving (2 Cor. 8:8-15)

Paul refused to appeal to his apostolic authority and exert any pressure that would "guilt" them into giving. He wanted their giving to be motivated by love so they would receive the full blessing that comes from such joyful giving. He used the testimony of the Macedonians to motivate the Corinthians to complete their offering, but now he appealed to the supreme motive for giving—**I am testing the genuineness of your love.** It is important to note that *love* begins and ends this section (v. 24). Their generosity would test and give concrete proof of their love.

Paul appealed to Christ as the supreme example of giving as an expression of love—**For you know the grace of our Lord Jesus Christ: Though He was rich, for your sake He became poor, so that by His poverty you might become rich.** *Became poor* translates a verb suggesting Paul wanted them to consider the condescension of the incarnation. Before the incarnation, Christ shared fully in the Father's glory (see John 17:5). He was infinitely rich. Grace was demonstrated when Christ laid aside all the riches of glory to take upon Himself human flesh and assume the role of the Suffering Servant (see Phil. 2:6-7). He did this for our sake and He did so when we were underserving sinners.

When we fully comprehend the gift that came from God's infinite love for us, a command to give should never be necessary.

Christ's act of self-giving love enabled believers to become rich. Our riches include forgiveness, eternal life, and the promise that one day we will share in the glory that Christ willingly laid aside. When we fully comprehend the gift that came from God's infinite love for us, a command to give should never be necessary. Thus Paul gave them his opinion that it is **profitable for you** to complete the task they had begun a year ago. Their generosity would not only relieve the suffering of the saints in Jerusalem, it would also allow them to demonstrate the genuineness of their love and further open them to the fullness of God's blessing. They had shown their desire to participate in the offering and now they must demonstrate the same zeal in the completion of the offering.

Giving is to be based on **what one has, not according to what he does not have.** Paul again stressed proportionate giving as was the case a year earlier (1 Cor. 16:2). Proportionate giving depends on the financial resources of the donor. The widow was used as an example by Jesus (Mark 12:43-44) because she gave out of her poverty whereas others were giving from their surplus. She gave all she had to live on. The problem with some who like to appeal to the story of the widow's mite to defend their level of giving is that they have more than adequate resources, particularly when they take into account the riches given to them through the poverty of Christ, and yet they want to give the widow's mite.

Verses 13-15, with its concluding appeal to the story of the miraculous provision of manna in the wilderness, may well have been prompted by criticism of the offering on the premise that relief for the poor would prove a hardship to the givers. Paul dismissed such a baseless excuse by asserting that such thinking is based on a lack of understanding of the resources God is prepared to make available. Like the miraculous manna, there will be neither too much nor too little. The goal of giving is never luxury for one and poverty for another, but equality. Equality is not to be understood in terms of socialism or communism, but in terms of the mutual sharing which exists in a healthy family. At the time of this letter, the surplus available to those in Corinth could help solve the problem of need that existed in Jerusalem because of the famine. In the course of time, it could become necessary for the Jerusalem church to meet a need of those in Corinth. Even if such an occasion never occurred, the Corinthians would profit from the prayers of those blessed by their generosity (9:14).

Left: A mite dating from the time of Tiberius. The reverse side shows three bound grain heads, which was a symbol of prosperity. There is also a Greek inscription that means "of Julia Augusta." Literally, that is "of Julia Caesar."

ILLUSTRATOR PHOTO/JAMES MCLEMORE (12/38/5)

Administered for the Glory of the Lord (2 Cor. 8:16-24)

Generous giving requires that it be administered in such a manner that it always glorifies the Lord. Paul momentarily departed from the principles of giving to clarify how the offering would be administered and who would be involved in transporting it to Jerusalem.

Generous giving requires that it be administered in such a manner that it always glorifies the Lord.

Paul first mentioned Titus who was well-known to the Corinthians. It is possible Titus may have delivered the first letter and had been instrumental in encouraging the Corinthians to begin the offering for the saints. He later had been sent with the painful letter and possibly had helped in the mediation that led to a successful resolution of the tension between Paul and the Corinthian community. Paul had requested that Titus return on this mission, but it had been unnecessary since he **went out to you by his own choice.** You may recall that the Corinthians had refreshed the spirit of Titus (7:13). Titus, Paul's **partner and coworker** was a natural choice since the Corinthians already had confidence in him.

Titus was accompanied by two brothers who are not mentioned by name (vv. 18,22). This first is described as **the brother who is praised throughout the churches for his gospel ministry.** Early commentators identified this brother with Luke, but that seems unlikely since this brother was famous for preaching the gospel. Besides his evangelistic ministry, he had been **appointed by the churches.** The second unnamed brother had been **tested** and had proven to be **diligent.** In this case, he was even more qualified to bear the offering because of his confidence in the Corinthians. It is apparent that the two brothers were well-known to the Corinthians and had their full confidence.

Paul spelled out the purposes for such elaborate precautions concerning the administration of the offering. The first was related to the **glory of the Lord Himself.** When givers reflect the generosity of the Lord, it is critical that the offering be handled in such a way that glory continues to be reflected upon the Lord. A second purpose was to illustrate Paul's desire to help the Corinthians in any way possible. The final reason was related to the church's testimony before the Lord and before men. Paul anticipated that the offering would be large, and he wanted to ensure that no one could find fault with how it was administered. He was aware that his critics would seize upon any administrative blunder to discredit him and his work.

It is worth underlining the verse, **For we are making provision for what is right, not only before the Lord but also before men.** It is foolish pride that would cause one to ignore the matter of public opinion based on the assertion that "my conscience is clear before the Lord." While we must maintain a clear conscience before the Lord, we must also maintain full openness and integrity before the world about how we handle God's resources.

While we must maintain a clear conscience before the Lord, we must also maintain full openness and integrity before the world about how we handle God's resources.

Giving as Ministry (2 Cor. 9:1-5)

Paul began chapter 9 by stating that it was unnecessary for him to write anything further about the ministry to the saints, yet he continued to write about it. This persistence on Paul's part demonstrates the vital nature of this ministry in the estimation of Paul. He had used the example of the Corinthians to motivate the giving of the churches in Macedonia. A failure on their part to be prepared when Paul and the messengers came to transport the offering would be embarrassing for everyone involved. Paul saw this offering as an event that would authenticate the validity of the ministry to the Gentiles.

Paul once again used the word *diakonia* (**ministry**) to describe the charitable offering for the saints in Jerusalem. We tend to think of ministry only in terms of our role of service in the church. Perhaps we would experience greater joy in our giving if we saw it as ministry. Giving is not a means of paying others to accomplish ministry, but is actual ministry to the Lord and to others.

Paul had told the churches of Macedonia that **Achaia** had been preparing for the offering for a year (1 Cor. 16). Achaia refers to the Roman province which included the Isthmus of Corinth and the land south of it. Paul may have been flattering the Corinthians by identifying the province with their city. The news about the preparations of the Corinthians had **stirred up most of them.**

His reason for sending Titus and the two brothers mentioned in 8:16-24 is made abundantly clear—**But I sent the brothers so our boasting about you in the matter would not prove empty.** The Macedonian delegates, when they came, would immediately know whether the Corinthians had followed through on their promise of a generous offering. The brothers would **arrange in advance** the promised generous gift, ensuring it was a gift and not something taken from them by force. According to 12:17-18, it appears that Paul has been accused of taking money from the Corinthians by force or deceit. He wanted it to be obvious to everyone that the offering flowed from grace and expressed the desire of the Corinthians.

Above: A seventh century A.D. bread stamp inscribed "eulogia Kuriou kai," menaing "the blessings of the Lord and ..."

ILLUSTRATOR PHOTO/DAVID ROGERS/JOSEPH A. CALLAWAY ARCHAEOLOGICAL MUSEUM/ THE SOUTHERN BAPTIST THEOLOGICAL SEMINARY/ LOUISVILLE, KY (13/3/1)

We often pray that others will be blessed, but then forget that we can be the instrument through which God conveys His blessing.

Gift translates the Greek word *eulogia,* a word that is not commonly used in this sense. The same word is used in the sense of "blessing" in 1 Corinthians 10:16. It is something that evokes thanksgiving. In the Greek translation of the Old Testament the word is used of the material gift that accompanies the blessing (Gen. 33:11 and 1 Sam. 25:27). We often pray that others will be blessed, but then forget that we can be the instrument through which God conveys His blessing. The Corinthian offering was both a ministry and a blessing. The same is true as we give today!

The Laws and Results of Joyous Giving (2 Cor. 9:6-15)

When our family moved to Virginia Beach to pastor First Baptist Norfolk, we purchased a home with a small but potentially beautiful front yard. I was a poor young pastor and thus I sprinkled the front yard with a small amount of seed. Needless to say, my dream of a plush green lawn was dashed. My dad, who was known for his green thumb, told me seed was inexpensive and should be spread liberally. I followed his advice and had a lush green lawn the next spring. Paul gave similar practical advice when it comes to living and giving.

1. *The Law of Sowing and Reaping.* Paul articulated four laws for effective giving and the first utilizes an agricultural metaphor. No one can refute the truth of this image taken from nature. All other things being equal, the quantity of the harvest will always be proportionate to the quantity of seed sown. Thus, Paul encouraged them to sow **generously,** literally "with blessing." In Hebrews 6:7 we are told that the fruitful land receives a blessing from God. When you sow blessing, you reap blessing.

2. *The Law of Cheerful Giving.* Paul declared, **Each person should do as he has decided in his heart—not reluctantly or out of necessity.** Giving is the outward expression of the inner state of one's heart. Thus, cheerful giving is never motivated by praise or fear of censure. *Reluctantly* speaks of giving grudgingly as if one is reluctant to part with what he considers to be his own. The words *out of necessity* have in mind the person who gives because he is afraid of what others may say. The bottom line is **for God loves a cheerful giver.** The word *loves* should be understood as "approves" or "rewards." This does not suggest that God doesn't love those who don't give. He loved us even while we were sinners. The point is that God is by nature a giver and He loves to see His children display His character in their giving.

God is by nature a giver and He loves to see his children display His character in their giving.

---

3. *The Law of Sufficiency.* We often give of ourselves and our money sparingly because we are afraid we might run out. Listen carefully to the law of sufficiency—**And God is able to make every grace overflow to you, so that in every way, always having everything you need, you may excel in every good work.** This is not simply a law about giving; it is a law about living. Notice that everything begins with God's ability. Further, you should notice the repetition of *every* and *everything* in this verse. When we have the desire to serve or give, God will make it possible out of his own grace. When we show grace to others, we will have an abundance of God's grace to enjoy ourselves and share with others.

4. *The Law of Multiplication.* Paul introduced and supported this principle in verse 9 by quoting from Psalm 112. The psalmist, looking at the traits of the

Above: Church of Multiplication at Tabgha

ISTOCK PHOTO

righteous, declared: "Happy is the man who fears the Lord, taking great delight in His commandments" (v. 1). In verse 3, the psalmist affirmed: "Wealth and riches are in his house, and his righteousness endures forever." However, it is to the first part of Psalm 112:9 that Paul paid particular attention:

"He distributes freely to the poor; his righteousness endures forever." The word *righteousness* embraces all acts of piety, but in the context it is a reference to almsgiving. Using words that sound almost like a benediction, Paul affirmed three things that God will do—(1) provide seed for the sower and bread for food; (2) multiply your seed; and (3) increase the harvest of your righteousness.

Using language from Isaiah 55:10—"seed to sow and food to eat"—Paul declared God to be the universal Provider. Notice that God provides for our needs (daily bread) but also additional resources for sowing or giving. If that wasn't enough, Paul declared that God will multiply the seed. When I read this promise I am reminded of Elisha multiplying the widow's oil (2 Kings 4:2-6), as well as the story of Jesus multiplying the five loaves and two fish (Matt. 14). Further, God promises to multiply the harvest of our righteousness. It is both good seed and good soil. God's purpose in providing and multiplying our seed is not to make us wealthy, but to give us a fruitful ministry of righteousness.

Paul concluded this section by looking at the results of generous giving. First, *giving enriches us*. Isn't it just like God to allow our giving to become a reciprocal blessing to us? Notice that in verse 11 Paul again repeated the words *every* and *all* to indicate the abundance of blessing we receive. Our giving enriches us by enabling us to thank God for His grace, by allowing us to meet the needs of others, and by building our faith. Notice we are enriched in every way **for all generosity.** Life really isn't about us!

Life really isn't about us!

Second, *giving allows us to meet needs of others*. The phrase translated **for the ministry of this service** brings together two theologically charged words to describe the collection for Jerusalem. One is *diakonia,* which means "service," and the other is *leitergeo,* which means "ritual service." This latter word is used in Luke 1:23 to speak of Zachariah's service as a priest in the temple. In other words, this offering was an act of worship which met the needs of others. Paul further underlined the theme of supplying needs through giving in verse 13, **in sharing with them and with others.** Paul was suggesting that the generosity of the Corinthians would enlarge the circle of believers. Generous giving creates a wonderful cycle of blessing.

Third, *giving expresses and inspires gratitude*. Thanksgiving to God dominated Paul's thought in this section and the idea is repeated three times (9:11,12,15). Thanksgiving is the attitude of the heart which distinguishes the believer from the non-believer (Rom. 1:21). Unbelievers fail to see that everything comes from the hand of God. Thus they fail to respond with thanksgiving. Believers, however, "enter His presence with thanksgiving" (Ps. 95:2) and bring their requests before Him "with thanksgiving" (Phil. 4:6).

An act of faith in sowing the seed provided by God became the instrument through which God extended and demonstrated His grace to the saints in Jerusalem. This demonstration of grace caused the saints in Jerusalem to give thanks. The language is more effusive in verse 12, where Paul declared that their gift not only met a need, **but is also overflowing in many acts of thanksgiving to God.**

Paul couldn't conclude this section without a final note of thanksgiving—**Thanks be to God for His indescribable gift.** The indescribable gift is the gift of God's Son. When we consider God's generosity in providing for redemption, it will produce a life of thanksgiving.

Fourth, *giving glorifies God.* If you thought the result of thanksgiving was wonderful, Paul has yet another treat in store for you. Through the proof of this service, **they will glorify God for your obedience to the confession of the gospel of Christ.** The sole end of man is to glorify God, and giving provides one way to do it.

This offering not only demonstrated the obedience of the Corinthian believers and met the needs of the saints in Jerusalem; it also caused the saints in Jerusalem to glorify God.

Give and Take

Paul urged us to excel in the grace of giving. Which is true of you? Put a T if describes how you give. Place an F is it's not true of you.

I feel like tithing is the least I can do in the area of giving. ____

An unexpected plea for financial help puts me in a bad mood. ____

Seeing homeless people on the street begging for money annoys me. ____

In addition to our church, I regularly support several charities. ____

I have been accused of being too generous. ____

I take the initiative in meeting others' needs. ____

I tend to believe we cannot afford to tithe or give. ____

Meeting others' needs fill me with joy. ____

I am annoyed when people don't thank me for my gifts. ____

I believe that God is glorified by my giving. ____

Nothing shows more clearly the genuineness of our confession of the gospel than our willingness to meet the needs of others. In contrast, nothing reveals shallow commitment like covetousness and its companion stinginess. Our giving has theological significance—it is an act of worship that glorifies God.

Nothing shows more clearly the genuineness of our confession of the gospel than our willingness to meet the needs of others. In contrast, nothing reveals shallow commitment like covetousness and its companion stinginess.

Personal Reflection

1. Share an example of one of the laws of giving at work in your own life.

2. Research indicates that a very small percentage of Christians tithe (give 10 percent) and fewer still give beyond the tithe. Why do you think people have such trouble embracing the principles of cheerful giving?

3. How have you experienced any of the results of giving in your own life? Would you share that with your class?

CHAPTER SIX

The Personal Challenges of Ministry

2 CORINTHIANS 10:1–13:14

When you were growing up did anyone ever remind you "life isn't always fair?" In response to challenges and difficult circumstances did someone tell you "life is tough?" My dad would often use these well-worn but truthful statements to encourage me when I felt I had been dealt with unfairly or wanted to give up on a difficult project.

If you have ever been involved in church ministry, you already know that it can be challenging. "Ministry would be fun if it wasn't for the people you have to deal with!" Have you ever felt that way? I have actually heard that sentiment voiced by people involved in ministry and, truthfully, I have probably felt that way myself from time to time. Ministry is about people and with people come challenges. Ministry can be messy and the challenges can be daunting, but the privilege and the commendation of the Lord make it all worth it.

In this last section, Paul addressed some of the personal challenges he faced as a minister, including having to deal with critics and the power struggles that occurred within the church. In response, he affirmed that his authority and assignment came from the Lord and that his goal was to build up the church. He desired the commendation of the Lord rather than the applause of men. In this final section of 2 Corinthians we will discover principles that will help us confront and overcome challenges in our service to the Lord.

Dealing with Unfair Criticism (2 Cor. 10:1-18)

When reading 2 Corinthians, you will notice a change of tone beginning in chapter 10. While a majority of the Corinthians had reaffirmed their loyalty to Paul, there must have been a recalcitrant minority who were still being unduly influenced by the claims of Paul's opponents. Since the issue was Paul's ministry and authority, he abandoned the "we" authorship and began with a personal appeal—**Now I, Paul, make a personal appeal.**

The first accusation that had been brought against Paul was that he was duplicitous—that he showed great boldness at a distance when he addressed them by letter, but was weak when he was with them in person. He responded to that accusation by referring to **the gentleness and graciousness of Christ.** Jesus referred to His own ministry in these very terms in Matthew 11:29. Thus, Paul affirmed that he was content to follow his Lord's example. Paul's critics had confused his meekness with weakness. Paul preferred to use gentle methods, but he could and would be more direct and confrontational if it proved to be necessary, and would do so on his next visit.

Secondly, it appears that some had accused Paul of ministering **in an unspiritual way.** It is apparent from both letters (see 1 Cor. 1:17) that some people judged Paul's preaching as lacking in power. They saw him as being deficient in the powerful gifts of the Spirit, and thus concluded that he was unspiritual while they were spiritual. Paul agreed that he was a mere man (**we live in the body**), but he strongly denied that he relied on fleshly weapons and human resources in his apostolic ministry. Paul's affirmation that he was mere man may also be an ironic reference to his allusion to their claim to be "super-apostles" (11:5).

Paul's ministry was a spiritual one which required both supernatural empowering and supernatural weapons. Worldly weapons might be things such as human ingenuity, cleverness, or eloquence. Spiritual weapons **are powerful through God** and are effective in demolishing **strongholds.** *Strongholds* refers to places where evil and disobedience are entrenched. No fleshly weapon can drive evil from its fortress. Any arrogant thought that is raised against the knowledge of God must be destroyed for man to submit himself fully to God. Thus, the prisoners of war in this battle are the thoughts and devices that are raised **against the knowledge of God.**

While Paul preferred the more gentle method of entreaty, he would **punish any disobedience** if necessary. The process he described fits well with the imagery of parenting Paul employed in the first letter (1 Cor. 4:14-21).

In defending his ministry, Paul simply said, **Look at what is obvious.** He was willing to let his ministry speak for itself. Paul didn't deny their claim to Christ's authority, he simply affirmed that he too belonged to Christ. It is possible that these super-apostles may have claimed to have seen and followed Jesus during His earthly ministry. Paul's credentials came by way of revelation of the risen Christ (Gal. 1:12).

When I was president of Southwestern Seminary, I consistently found that attempting to defend my actions was of little value. Such a tactic simply created more rhetoric. It was always a better strategy to let the work speak for itself. I highly recommend Paul's strategy to anyone in ministry.

Paul was reluctant to boast about his credentials, but was willing to do so if necessary for the good of the community. Therefore, he boasted in what should have been apparent to them—the Lord chose Paul to found and build up the church in Corinth (2 Cor. 10:8). The very existence of the church in Corinth was evidence that God worked mightily through him (see 12:11-12).

Paul again turned to the persistent argument that his letters were strong and his personal presence week and he handled it in a somewhat ironic way (10:9-11). They were hearing this by means of a letter and thus (tongue in cheek) he doesn't want to terrify them with his letter. In truth, his opponents were right about the power of Paul's letters, since the tearful letter had led most of the Corinthians to repent and affirm their love for Paul. They were wrong, however, about his personal presence and this they would see in his impending visit.

Paul next turned his attention to the assignment he had been given by the Lord as the only appropriate sphere for boasting (vv. 12-18). This section begins with a rather ironic confession—he was weak when it came to comparing himself with the super-apostles who commended themselves by self-praise which was unsupported by any evidence. In truth, self-praise is hollow praise and thus Paul looked only for the praise of God in the field in which He had been assigned by God.

The boasting of Paul's opponents knew no bounds, but Paul refused to boast beyond the **measure** of the ministry given to him by God (v. 13). Paul used the Greek *kanon* which refers to a reed used for measurement. His ministry was to the Gentiles and specifically to serve as a pioneer missionary or church planter among them. He did not desire to build on another man's foundation (see Rom. 15:20). Under God's assignment, Corinth came within his sphere of ministry. Paul had God's authority in Corinth and by implication the false apostles had none. Paul, unlike the false apostles, was not bragging **beyond measure about other people's labors.** Paul's hope was that the faith of the Corinthians would be strengthened so that he would feel the freedom to go on to other fields and thus have a greatly enlarged ministry to regions beyond them.

Paul used the word ***boasts*** frequently in this section because of the exaggerated boasting of his opponents. He now made it clear that his boasting was not about what he had accomplished, but about what the Lord accomplished through him. The apostle employed a quotation from Jeremiah 9:23-24, which had already been employed in 1 Corinthians 1:31. Paul's ultimate desire in ministry was to have God's approval (2 Cor. 10:18).

When facing critics, we must let the evidence speak for itself. We don't need to defend ourselves if we know we have the approval of the One who assigned us the ministry task. Like Paul, the motivating factor of our ministry should be God's approval.

The motivating factor of our ministry should be God's approval.

Dealing with False Teachers (2 Cor. 11:1-15)

Paul had just affirmed that there is no value in praising oneself, but in his present circumstances such **foolishness** was necessary because his love for the Corinthians was matched only by their naiveté. If boasting was required to keep them loyal to Christ; then boast he would. His boasting was motivated by **godly jealousy.** Paul employed the image of marriage, an image consistently used in the Old Testament to speak of God's love for His people. He had promised them to Christ and he was determined to present them as a pure virgin to their groom.

Paul's fear was that, as the serpent deceived Eve, the minds of the Corinthians would be corrupted and they would depart **from a complete and pure devotion to Christ.** False teachers often attempt to improve on the simplicity of the gospel by either subtraction or addition. Their primary tool is subtlety and deception just like the serpent in the garden.

What the Corinthians had put up with **splendidly** was a message that included **another Jesus,** inspired by **a different spirit,** and which was in essence a **different gospel** than the one they accepted. It seems likely that Paul's opponents were adding works to the gospel which would in essence nullify the true gospel. It is still true that most heretical teaching begins with an unbiblical view of Jesus and that all other religious systems depend on good works.

Most heretical teaching begins with an unbiblical view of Jesus.

Apparently, some Corinthians were in danger of being corrupted by such teaching because they were enamored with the supposed credentials and powerful rhetoric of the **"super-apostles."** In essence, they were trying to buttress their case by name-dropping. It is possible that *super-apostles* was Paul's ironical way of referring to men who were, in truth, not apostles at all (see 2 Cor. 12:11).

These men apparently belittled Paul's ministry on two counts, his lack of trained speaking ability and his failure to take compensation for his ministry. Paul admitted to being **untrained in public speaking.** He employed a word used for those who lacked professional or technical training. In Acts 4:13, Peter and John were dubbed "uneducated and untrained men." In other words, they had no training in biblical exegesis like the rabbis. Paul admitted that he was an apostle and not a professional orator. He did not consider his lack of speaking ability to be a detriment to his ministry since he relied on the Spirit to give expression to spiritual truths (1 Cor. 2:13). It is the clarity of the truth taught rather than oratorical ability which possesses power.

It is the clarity of the truth taught rather than oratorical ability which possesses power.

Some in Corinth were apparently offended that Paul refused to accept compensation from them, but accepted support from Macedonia while ministering in Corinth (2 Cor. 11:7-11). His detractors were pointing to his lack of pay as evidence that he was not an authentic apostle. Paul's motives for not receiving money from Corinth were pure and well thought out. Paul had already offered a detailed explanation of his reason for not accepting money from them in his first letter (1 Cor. 9:4-18). He fully acknowledged the right of the minister to be compensated for his work, but he had chosen to forego his right so that his actions would not hinder the gospel. Paul apparently knew that the immature Corinthians would suspect him of being a charlatan if he received money from them.

Paul ironically inquired as to whether he had committed a sin by humbling himself so that they could be exalted. In other words, he wanted them to be able to give full attention to the message and thus become children of the rightful King. To provide his ministry at no charge in Corinth was almost like robbing from other churches. They should have been mature enough to desire to pay their own fair share. He had chosen to work as a tent maker and had received a gift from Macedonia—a likely reference to the gift from Philippi (Phil. 4:15).

Verse 10 begins with a solemn assertion—**As the truth of Christ is in me**—and verse 11 ends with another—**God knows I do** to indicate how important this issue was to Paul. As long as he ministered in Achaia (Corinth), he would continue this policy out of his great love for them. His practice would provide no opportunity for his intrusive critics to claim equality with Paul in this matter (v. 12). His motives are pure, theirs are not.

This section is strongly worded because false doctrine is both subtle and dangerous. Paul described them as **false apostles, deceitful workers, disguising themselves as apostles of Christ.** They were false apostles not "super-apostles," they were workers of iniquity who had the outward appearance of an apostle but were actually servants of Satan. Their deceptive behavior was no surprise, for Satan masquerades as an angel of light. Satan never shows himself for who he is and sin never shows itself for what it is.

Ultimately **their destiny will be according to their works.** It is a clear teaching of Scripture that no matter how much the wicked seem to prosper, their end will be based on God's fair and impartial judgment. Jesus indicated that when the Son of man will come in His glory, "He will reward each according to what he has done" (Matt. 16:27). These are strong and frightening words, but there can be no compromise when it comes to truth.

There can be no compromise when it comes to truth.

Dealing with Suffering for Christ (2 Cor. 11:16-33)

Paul once again returned to his "foolish" boasting. The first several verses of this section are filled with irony. Since Paul's opponents boasted in the flesh and some in Corinth were so gullible as to be influenced by their boasting, Paul would employ their tactic against them. It was clearly against the grain for Paul to defend himself with self-praise, but he was willing to do so to help those who were wavering in their support of him.

Such boasting is not what the Lord would do; it is certainly no fruit of the Spirit. But in the case of those being misled by the false apostles, it became a negative necessity. Since his opponents were boasting from a human perspective, Paul would follow suit. You can hear the irony drip from the assertion—**For you, being so wise, gladly put up with fools!**

These false apostles were both braggarts and tyrants whose goal was to enslave the Corinthians. The phrase ***enslaves you*** translates the same verb used in Galatians 2:4 where Paul spoke of the Judaizers, early Christian Jews who wanted to require Christians to keep the law in its entirety. The false teachers in Corinth may have had some of the same legalistic tendencies. It is also possible that Paul was simply making a general reference to the desire of the super-apostles to make the Corinthians fully dependent on them. In either case, they were doing it at the expense of the Corinthians. The word ***devours*** is used of the Pharisees who "devour widows' houses" (Luke 20:47). The false teachers captured the Corinthians like birds and hit them in the face. To hit someone in the face was a mark of greatest disrespect and thus is a symbol of humiliating treatment. The stock-in-trade of all false teachers is to make their followers fully dependent on them throughout whatever tactics they deem viable.

Spiritual Abuse

In Paul's warning to the Corinthians of false teachers, we can glean that he considered their tactics to be akin to spiritual abuse. List the verbs in 11:20 that Paul employed to characterize the actions of these false teachers:

What are the tell-tale signs of spiritual abuse to watch for today?

The phrase ***I say this to our shame: We have been weak*** is likely pure irony where Paul was again representing himself as weak in terms of taking advantage of and abusing the Corinthians like these men they seemed to prefer. Now Paul declared that he was taking off the gloves when it comes to foolish boasting.

In the lengthy listing that follows in verses 22-27, the two major categories are lineage and ministry experience. In verse 22, Paul compared his lineage, line by line, and showed that he was lacking in no quarter. Paul didn't attack their claim to be ministers of Christ, but trumped it with superior credentials, all the while affirming that he was **talking like a madman.** In other words, it is sheer madness to boast in one's service of Christ since all such service is a gift of God's grace. Paul's list is impressive, including more numerous

evangelistic campaigns, more imprisonments, and more beatings that brought him to the point of death on several occasions. He then listed five beatings from the Jews and three with rods from Roman authorities. Deuteronomic Law allowed for a maximum of 40 lashes (Deut. 25:1-3), but in the desire to avoid going beyond the law they had settled on 39 lashes. The whip had three thongs and thus it took 13 strokes to satisfy the requirement of 39 lashes.

It is sheer madness to boast in one's service of Christ since all such service is a gift of God's grace.

Paul continued his litany of suffering with shipwrecks, a night and a day lost at sea, **dangers from rivers, dangers from robbers,** dangers from Jews, **dangers from the Gentiles, dangers in the city,** and **dangers in the open country.** Paul's life of

Left: St. Paul's Bay at Malta

ILLUSTRATOR PHOTO/ BOB SCHATZ (19/32/16)

Below: Replica of a Roman whip

ISTOCK PHOTO

ministry was marked by hard work and hardships which frequently led to physical privation.

But these physical sufferings were nothing in comparison to **the daily pressure on me: my care for all the churches.** Anyone who has engaged in ministry can identify with Paul's conclusion that his love and concern from the church was the most arduous part of ministry. The minister so identifies with his people that he empathizes with the weak and experiences moral indignation when someone is caused to stumble.

Wanted: Super Apostle

Pretend you are on an apostle search team and looking for someone for a leadership position in your church. What credentials listed in 2 Corinthians 11:22-30 could persuade you to consider him as a candidate?

Which, if any, would cause you to eliminate or re-consider him as a candidate?

Verse 30 ends the section of "foolish" boasting with a paradoxical twist. In setting out to counter the claims of the false apostles, he had boasted in the things they would find demeaning—**I will boast about my weaknesses.** The preceding list was so overwhelming that he realized someone might think Paul was exaggerating and thus He called on **the God and Father of the Lord Jesus Christ** as his witness.

It appears that this solemn oath reminded him of an incident that occurred at the very outset of his ministry. King Aretas had attempted to have him arrested in Damascus and God preserved His life for ongoing ministry (v. 32).

Ministry is not for the faint of heart for it will entail suffering of varying kinds and varying degrees, but it is for the pure in heart. God will receive glory when we faithfully minister in His name.

Ministry is not for the faint of heart for it will entail suffering of varying kinds and varying degrees, but it is for the pure in heart.

Finding God's Strength in Our Weaknesses (2 Cor. 12:1-13)

Before Paul could fully leave behind his foolish boasting, he would consider one other area where his opponents seemed to be attacking him, finding him to be deficient—**visions and revelations.** It is possible that some were denying

Paul's apostolic title because it was based on a vision on the Damascus road. Further, it is possible that some were demeaning Paul for his lack of powerful visionary experiences. The Book of Acts makes it abundantly clear that Paul indeed had visionary experiences subsequent to his Damascus road experience. He had a vision of Ananias' visit (9:12), the vision that led him to Macedonia (16:9), the vision in Jerusalem on his first visit after his conversion (22:17-21), at Jerusalem during his last visit (23:11), and a final one on his voyage to Rome (27:23-26). But the vision mentioned here is not to be identified with any of those, and certainly not with the Damascus road experience. The Damascus road experience would have been 20 years ago, not 14 (2 Cor. 12:2).

Paul was so reluctant to speak of visions and revelations that he identified himself impersonally as **a man in Christ.** This man was **caught up,** which underlines that the initiative was with God and not with Paul. The heavens were variously enumerated in Judaism, but the phrase **the third heaven** probably serves to emphasize the supreme blessedness of this visionary experience. Paul indicated that in this moment of ecstasy he was not sure whether he was **in the body or out of the body.** It was such an overwhelming experience only God knew that. In paradise he **heard inexpressible words, which a man is not allowed to speak.** Notice the emphasis is on what Paul heard rather than what he saw. That which he heard, he was not allowed to speak.

Below: Obverse side of a coin of Aretas IV king of Nabatea. The reign of Aretas (9 B.C.–A.D. 41) is well documented. We know more about his reign than any other of the Nabatean rulers. About 80 percent of the extant Nabatean coinage comes from his reign. Early in his reign, Aretas lost his source of silver, so for a while he issued bronze coins—which were unacceptable to the Jerusalem temple since it accepted only silver coinage.

ILLUSTRATOR PHOTO/ JAMES MCLEMORE/ JERRY VARDAMAN COLLECTION (14/10/14)

Bottom: The traditional site where Paul was let down out of the window and over the wall at Damascus.

ILLUSTRATOR PHOTO/ BOB SCHATZ (8/41/16)

In other words, it was not a source for his preaching and teaching ministry. It is possible some of his opponents were using their supposed visions as the source for their teaching. A visionary experience is an unreliable source, since by its very nature; no one else can verify it.

Paul could not imagine using this visionary experience to add to his personal resume. In the telling of this event, it is like he was boasting about someone else. Therefore, he would be content to boast in his weaknesses. If he were to boast of his experience, he would not be lying, but he refused to boast further in his visionary experience and was comfortable with his converts and detractors judging him based on what they saw and heard from him.

Paul's experience was so extraordinary he could have been tempted to exalt himself. But there is no danger he would do that because the Lord gave him a **thorn in the flesh ... a messenger of Satan to torment** him so that he would not exalt himself. There is no consensus on the nature of the thorn in the flesh. Most commentators believe Paul was referring to some sort of physical ailment that was embarrassing and sometimes debilitating. Those following such a view will connect this passage to Galatians 4:13-15. Other commentators argue that *flesh* here refers to the lower nature of man which is still susceptible to painful experiences and tempting thoughts. In that case, Paul might have been speaking of spiritual pride that could come from successful ministry or powerful ecstatic experiences. The reference to the *messenger of Satan* could work in either case since Satan is sometimes portrayed as one who is an agent of physical disease (Job 2:5) and he is also presented as the adversary who interferes with the spread of the gospel (1 Thess. 2:18).

Paul, in similar fashion to the Lord in the Garden of Gethsemane, prayed three times for the removal of the thorn. His prayer was not answered as expected, but in a more wonderful way—**My grace is sufficient for you, for power is perfected in weakness.** When we are discouraged, humiliated, or beaten down, we need to remember that we are unworthy objects of unmerited favor. Therefore, with Paul we can declare **I will most gladly boast all the more about my weaknesses, so that Christ's power may reside in me ... For when I am weak, then I am strong.**

Apologetically Paul sighed, **I have become a fool; you forced it on me.** There should never have been any need for Paul to defend himself; the Corinthians should have come to his defense. The word ***nothing*** in verse 11 probably reflects the false apostles' evaluation of Paul. Paul admitted that such an assessment would be true if one took into account the fact that everything that made him worthy of being an apostle was given him by the grace of God. The signs of an authentic apostle were performed in their midst in challenging circumstances by Paul. Based on all this evidence, how could some assert that Paul treated them worse than other churches? The only way they were treated worse, ironically, is that he did not personally burden them.

Paul's Third Visit and Final Remarks (2 Cor. 12:14–13:13)

Twice in this final section Paul spoke of his impending visit (12:14; 13:1). He promised that his visit would be no burden, for he had no interest in their money; he wanted them. He was like a father to them and would willingly **spend and be spent** for their good. There was no limit to Paul's love; and it is sad that they had been stingy in returning his affection. As hard as it is to imagine, some were still implying that Paul took advantage of them by deceit, perhaps in sending messengers to deal with the final stages of their contribution to the Jerusalem fund. But these messengers demonstrated the same integrity and spirit as Paul.

Verse 19 is a key verse for understanding the motivation for authentic ministry. Nothing spoken by Paul in person or written in this letter had as its purpose defending Paul's ministry; everything was done **for building** them **up.** He repeated this same sentiment in 13:10, where he declared that everything he had written in this letter has a singular purpose of allowing him not to use severe means to bring correction, but the authority of Christ to build them up. The strength of this letter is explained by his fear that when he arrived he would discover both disorderly behavior and sexual misconduct.

Paul opened the final chapter with a warning, based on Deuteronomy 19:15 and requiring **two or three witnesses.** His third visit would be the decisive visit, and if repentance was not clearly evidenced by those who had sinned, Paul would not be lenient. If they were looking for evidence that Christ was speaking through him, it would be abundantly clear on this visit. Christ was **crucified in weakness** by the world's standards, but **He lives by God's power.** Those who are united with Christ in his passion will also experience the power of His resurrection. Paul's ministry would display resurrection power.

Paul's visit would be like a final exam for the Corinthians. Rather than asking whether Christ was speaking in Paul, they needed to ask themselves if Christ was living in them. The apostle did not believe nor desire that they fail the test. He was sure that he was the genuine article and was praying that they would prove to be the same—not to vindicate his own apostolic authority, but for their good. Paul could not act contrary to the truth and thus he gladly accepted his weakness if it led to their maturity.

This letter and his coming visit both have a singular motive—**that when I am there I will not use severity, in keeping with the authority the Lord gave me for building up and not for tearing down.** Characteristically, Paul ended with a powerful benediction that sought joy, encouragement, unity, and peace. He brought them greetings from other believers and then prayed, **The grace of the Lord Jesus Christ, and the love of God, and the fellowship of the Holy Spirit be with all of you."** Amen!

Personal Reflection

1. In dealing with criticism, why is it so difficult to let our actions speak for themselves?

2. Identify times when you depended on your own natural ability to accomplish supernatural ministry? What is the result of that?

3. Why are there so many challenges to ministry and why so many critics?

4. Give examples of areas where you discovered that your weakness was actually a strength?